gage Cornerstones

CANADIAN LANGUAGE ARTS

Anthology 4a

gage EDUCATIONAL PUBLISHING COMPANY
A DIVISION OF CANADA PUBLISHING CORPORATION
Vancouver · Calgary · Toronto · London · Halifax

Canadian Cataloguing in Publication Data

McClymont, Christine
Cornerstones Canadian language arts 4a

ISBN 0-7715-1200-7

1. Readers (Elementary).   I. Lashmar, Patrick.   II. Title.

PE1121.M326 1997   428.6   C97-931464-X

Permissions Editor: Elizabeth Long

Researchers: Todd Mercer, Monika Croydon

Cover Illustration: Laurie Lafrance

Acknowledgments

Every reasonable effort has been made to trace ownership of copyrighted material. Information that would enable the publisher to correct any reference or credit in future editions would be appreciated.

1 "You Meet Your Friend" by Kassia from *The Little Book of Friendship* selected by Caroline Walsh (New York: Kingfisher, 1995). © 1995 Larousse PLC. Reprinted with permission. / **2-4** Excerpt from *The Best Friends Book* by Arlene Erlbach, copyright © 1995. Used with permission from Free Spirit Publishing Inc., Minneapolis, MN. All rights reserved. / **8-17** *The Moccasin Goalie* by William Roy Brownridge (Victoria: Orca Book Publishers, 1995). © 1995 William Roy Brownridge. / **22** "When My Friend Anita Runs" by Grace Nichols from *Give Yourself a Hug* (London: Puffin Books/Penguin Books, Ltd., 1994). © Grace Nichols 1994. Reprinted with permission of Curtis Brown Ltd., London. / **24-29** "The Southpaw" by Judith Viorst from *Free To Be . . . You And Me* by Marlo Thomas (Whitby: McGraw-Hill Ryerson Limited, 1994). © 1974 by Judith Viorst. Reprinted with permission of Lescher & Lescher, Ltd., New York. / **32** "Lisa" by Beverly McLoughland from *Through Our Eyes, Poems and Pictures About Growing Up* selected by Lee Bennett Hopkins (Boston: Little Brown & Company, 1992). © Beverly McLoughland. / **34-41** *Lights For Gita* by Rachna Gilmore (Toronto: Second Story Press, 1994). Reprinted with permission of Second Story Press. / **45** "My Olympic Tabby Cat" by Lola Sneyd from CRICKET MAGAZINE (November, 1994), Vol. 22, No. 3. Reprinted with permission of the author. / **48-51** "Animals Make Good Friends" from *Animals and Us* by Sara Corbett (Chicago: Children's Press, 1995). / **54-59** "Hunting With Raven" by Diana C. Conway. Reprinted with permission of CRICKET MAGAZINE (January, 1996), Vol. 23, No. 5. © 1996 Diana C. Conway. / **62** "Limericks" by X. J. Kennedy from *The Big Book of Our Planet* by Ann Durell, Jean Craighead George, and Katherine Paterson (New York: Penguin/Dutton Children's Books, 1993). © 1993 X. J. Kennedy. Reprinted with permission of the author. / **63** "The Whales Off Wales" from *One Winter Night in August* by X. J. Kennedy (New York: Atheneum, 1995). © 1975 by X. J. Kennedy. Reprinted with permission of Curtis Brown, Ltd. / **64-71** Excerpts from *Canadian Endangered Species* by Colleayn O. Mastin (Kamloops: Grasshopper Book Publishing, 1995). © 1995 Colleayn O. Mastin. Reprinted with permission of the author. / **74-79** "Wolf Watcher" by Sami Antaki and Jenny Ryon from WILD MAGAZINE (April 1996), Vol. 1, No. 5. Reprinted with permission of the authors. / **82** "Our Hamster's Life" by Kit Wright from *Rabbitting On* (East Sussex: Wayland Publishers Ltd., 1991). Reprinted with permission of HarperCollins Publishers, London. / **86-95** From *A Dog Came, Too* by Ainslie Manson (Toronto: Groundwood Books/Douglas & McIntyre, 1992). © 1992 by Ainslie Manson. Edited by permission of the author. / **100-104** From *Maps and Mapping*, text adapted from Barbara Taylor. © Grisewood & Dempsey Ltd., 1992. First American edition 1992. Reprinted with permission of Larousse Kingfisher Chambers, New York. / **116-117** "Trip to the Seashore" by Lois Simmie from *Auntie's Knitting a Baby*

© 1984, published by Douglas & McIntyre. Edited and reprinted with the permission of Douglas & McIntyre. / **118-123** "Going Underground" by Diane Bailey and Drew McKibben from WILD MAGAZINE (April 1996), Vol. 1, No. 5. Reprinted with permission of the authors. / **126** "This Canada" by Maxine Tynes from *Save the World For Me* (Porters Lake, NS: Pottersfield Press, 1991). Reprinted with permission of the author. / **130-132** "How Eagle Man created the islands of the Pacific Coast" by C. J. Taylor from *How we saw the world: nine native stories of the way things began* (Toronto: Tundra Books, 1993) © 1993 C. J. Taylor. / **134-137** "The Spider Weaver," a Japanese story retold by Florence Sakade from *Japanese Children's Favorite Stories*, edited by Florence Sakade (Boston, MA: Charles E. Tuttle Co., Inc, 1958). Reprinted with permission. / **140-143** "The Man Who Could Transform Himself" from *Wonder Tales from Around the World* by Heather Forest (August House, 1995). © 1995 Heather Forest. Reprinted with permission of the publisher. / **144-151** Reprinted with the permission of Hyperion Books for Children. From *The Hummingbird's Gift*. Text © 1994 Stefan Czernecki and Timothy Rhodes; illustrations © 1994 Stefan Czernecki.

Photo Credits

v McKibben and Bailey. Books for Children, 1994; **vi middle right** © EFA/First Light; **bottom** Roy Morsch/First Light; **1** Stephen Wilkes/The Image Bank; **20** B. Harder; **43 top left** Gary Farber/The Image Bank; **43 top middle** Tony Stone Images; **43 middle left** Oliver Benn/Tony Stone Images; **43 middle right** Chad Ehlers/Tony Stone Images; **43 bottom right** Paul Harris/Tony Stone Images; **47, 73** Dave Starrett; **48 left, 50 left** Superstock International Inc.; **48 right** Photo Researchers, Inc.; **49 top left** Victor Englebert; **49 middle** Tony Stone Images; **49 bottom right, 51 bottom right** Odyssey Productions; **50-51 middle** R.C. Simpson/Valan Photos; **51 top right** Joe McDonald/Visuals Unlimited; **51 middle** Mike Beedell/Canada In Stock/Ivy Images; **74 right** Thomas Kitchin/Victoria Hurst; **74-79** Jenny Ryon; **98** Cory Flahr; **99** David Manson; **133** Norman Keene; **118, 119 top, 120 right, 121-123** Paul Whitfield; **119 bottom, 120 left** McKibben and Bailey. Books for Children, 1994.

Illustrations

7, 105 Dan Hobbs; **19, 102, 103** Margo Davies Leclair/Visual Sense; **31, 81** Dayle Dodwell; **46 left** Marion Stuck; **46 right, 61, 73, 114** Jun Park; **53, 115** Steve Attoe; **64-71** Jan Sovak; **84-85** Robert Johannsen; **95** Jack McMaster; **97 middle right** James Hill; **100, 101 right, 104** Larousse PLC; **128-129** Martin Springett; **138, 139** David Bathurst; **152** Clarence Porter; **144-151** Stefan Czernecki.

Special thanks to Luigi Iannacci's grade 4/5 class at St. Michael's School, Dufferin-Peel RCSSB, for the quotations on page 4-5.

Cornerstones Development Team

HERE ARE THE PEOPLE WHO WORKED HARD TO MAKE THIS BOOK EXCITING FOR YOU!

WRITING TEAM

Christine McClymont
Patrick Lashmar
Dennis Strauss
Patricia FitzGerald-Chesterman
Cam Colville
Stephen Hurley
Oksana Kuryliw
Caroline Lutyk

GAGE EDITORIAL

Joe Banel
Caroline Cobham
Rivka Cranley
David MacDonald
Darleen Rotozinski

GAGE PRODUCTION

Anna Kress
Bev Crann

DESIGN, ART DIRECTION & ELECTRONIC ASSEMBLY

Pronk&Associates

ADVISORY TEAM

Connie Fehr Burnaby SD, BC
Elizabeth Sparks Delta SD, BC
Joan Alexander St. Albert PSSD, AB
Carol Germyn Calgary B of E, AB
Cathy Sitko Edmonton Catholic SD, AB
Laura Haight Saskatoon SD, SK
Linda Nosbush Prince Albert SD, SK
Maureen Rodniski Winnipeg SD, MB
Luigi Iannacci Dufferin-Peel RCSSB, ON
Cathy Saytar Dufferin-Peel RCSSB, ON
Jan Adams London B of E, ON
John Cassano York Region B of E, ON
Carollynn Desjardins Nipissing RCSSB, ON
David Hodgkinson Waterloo County B of E, ON
Michelle Longlade Halton RCSSB, ON
Sharon Morris Metropolitan Separate SB, ON
Heather Sheehan Metropolitan Separate SB, ON
Ruth Scott Brock University, ON
Elizabeth Thorn Nipissing University, ON
Jane Abernethy Chipman & Fredericton SD, NB
Darlene Whitehouse-Sheehan Chipman & Fredericton SD, NB
Carol Chandler Halifax Regional SB, NS
Martin MacDonald Strait Regional Board, NS
Ray Doiron University of PEI, PE
Robert Dawe Avalon East SD, NF
Margaret Ryall Avalon East SD, NF

Contents

MY Friends and I

You Meet Your Friend

Poem by Kassia

You meet your friend,
    your face
Brightens—you have struck
    gold.

1

BEFORE READING

•

Before you read "Best Friends," look at the title and the subheadings. Who are the two best friends in the article? Find the part where Brian talks about his friend, and then the part where Osman talks about *his* friend.

ARTICLE BY
Arlene Erlbach

PICTURES BY
Kevin Ghiglione

Best Friends

You laugh with your best friend. You cry with your best friend. You share secrets you'd never tell anyone else. Your best friend is sometimes closer to you than any of your family members. A best friend can be a second self.

Yet sometimes your best friend makes you mad. Then you swear you'll never speak again – no matter what! You usually make up. Some people even remain best friends when they grow up.

Brian and Osman talk about being best friends

Brian "People sometimes think I'm older than Osman because I'm so much bigger than he is. We're the same age, but I'm big for my age and Osman is small. My mom says we look like Mutt and Jeff—two old-fashioned comic strip characters.

"I liked Osman right from the minute I met him. I found out that he's into football, basketball, and collecting comic books—the things I like best. We're both wild about comic books. We both have stacks of them. Someday our comics will be worth lots of money, and Osman and I will both be rich.

"I go over to Osman's house more than he comes to mine. His older married sister lives with them. She has a baby, and Osman has to watch the baby for her when she works. I don't mind. We still have fun together. Even when Osman doesn't have to watch the baby, I still like going to his house. He has a basketball hoop on his garage, and I love playing basketball. We can play basketball for hours and talk, and it feels like we've only been playing a few minutes.

Osman (left)
and Brian (right)

"Osman's parents speak Spanish, not English, so I can't understand them. They're probably not talking about anything I'd be interested in anyhow. And maybe Osman can teach me Spanish. That way we'll have a language that's secret from certain people.

"Sometimes people wonder how it feels to be so much bigger than your best friend. It doesn't matter to me at all. What matters is what kind of person somebody is. Size doesn't count."

Osman "I like Brian because he tells good jokes, he collects comic books, and he likes basketball. Also, he's a lot nicer than most other kids I know. When we're playing basketball, he doesn't hog the ball or make sure he gets it first. Sometimes kids do that to me because I'm small.

"When Brian and I play basketball, we like to make believe that we're big stars, like Michael Jordan or Larry Bird. I don't do that with other guys—maybe they'd think it was dumb. Or maybe other guys pretend that they're basketball stars, too, when they're playing and don't admit it to anyone. They'd think that other guys would think that was dorky. Still, I won't tell any other guys that we do that.

Brian (left) and Osman (right)

TIP: Best friendships are special

"Brian and I like video games. He has Nintendo and I have Sega. I read all the game magazines, so I know lots of strategies not many other kids know. I've even learned some strategies myself because I play a lot. Brian is the only person I discuss new game strategies with. I don't want everyone to know about them. That way, they can get to higher levels sooner than we do, and I want us to be the first ones to reach them.

"One thing I wish is that I could go to Brian's house more, but I can't. I need to baby-sit for my nephew. It doesn't matter that much. A best friend is a best friend, no matter where you see him."

They take time.

Brian and Osman told you a lot about each other in the article. Would you like to be friends with Osman, with Brian, or with both of them? Why?

Understanding the Article

- One reason Brian and Osman are friends is that they like doing the same things. They have a lot in common. Make a list of four things they like to do together.

- Osman has to baby-sit a lot. How do Brian and Osman make sure this doesn't cause problems in their friendship?

- What do you think is the best thing about having a friend?

Interview Some Best Friends

You can find out more about best friends by interviewing them. That's what author Arlene Erlbach did: she talked to Brian about Osman, and to Osman about Brian, and wrote down what they told her. Choose a pair of friends your age or older and ask them a few questions like these:

How did you meet each other?
What things do you like to do together?
Do you ever have fights?
How do you make up?

Think of two more questions you might want to ask.

Take notes of the answers the pair of friends tell you.
If you like, you could write an article just like *Best Friends*.

TIP If your school has a web site, create a page that asks friendship questions.

High Score for Good Reading!

Make a Good Friends Scrapbook

Wouldn't you like to look through a book of memories? Think of a friend you have, or one you would like to have. You can fill a scrapbook with things that remind you of good times you've had together. First make a list of some things to save in your Good Friends Scrapbook.

Imagine how you'll feel when you're an adult and you open a scrapbook from the age you are now!

Suggestions for your scrapbook:

- ticket stubs from a movie you saw together
- pictures of sports stars or singers you both like
- letters, postcards, and e-mail messages you sent each other

Friendship Collage

Read the quotes on pages 4 and 5 from students your age. Do you agree with their ideas about what makes a best friend?

Get together with a small group or the whole class and add your ideas about friends.

Turn your ideas into a big Friendship Collage. Find pictures in magazines. You could add photographs and drawings of yourself and your friends.

A Good Friend...

makes me laugh

always understands me

knows when I'm just kidding

This is a true story. It happened when the author was about your age. As you read it, think about the "old days on the Prairies."

• What things were the same as now?

• What things were different?

THE
Moccasin
Goalie

STORY AND PICTURES BY
William Roy Brownridge

A LONG TIME AGO when I was a boy, my family lived on the Prairies in a small town called Willow. The winters there were very cold, with the wind blowing the deep snow into huge drifts. My friends and I didn't mind. This was our favourite time of year. Cold temperatures meant ice, and ice meant hockey!

I had four best friends. We lived for hockey.

Anita had long braids that flew out behind her when she skated. Marcel was big and quiet and good at sports. Then there was the tough little guy we nicknamed "Petou." And finally there was my dog Bingo, who always tried to steal the puck.

I was the goalie. I had a twisted leg and foot, so I couldn't wear skates. But my leather moccasins were just fine. I was quick and could slide across the goalmouth really fast. They called me "Moccasin Danny."

Before the really cold weather brought ice to our rink, we played road hockey right on Main Street in front of the Red & White store. Pieces of firewood or old overshoes marked our goals. We didn't have streetlights, and sometimes after dark we'd play by the light spilling from the store windows.

Often, on stormy days, Mom let us play inside with a soft ball of sponge rubber.

As time went by, we became more and more impatient for the day when we could play real hockey.

When winter finally arrived, the rink was the centre of attention. The men and big boys began the flooding. We watched as the ice became thick and smooth. Later, our job would be to keep it clear of snow. We spent hours scraping and sweeping so we could drop the puck on beautiful gleaming ice.

Dad said we had hockey on the brain. Mom said she heard me talking about hockey in my sleep.

One morning there was a surprise at the rink. Mr. Matteau gathered us together.

"We're going to have a hockey team. It'll be called the Wolves," he said. "I'll be your coach, and today I choose the team. What do you say, boys?"

We shouted and screamed with glee. This was going to be hockey heaven.

Everyone was silent as Mr. Matteau began reading out the names for the new team. Marcel was first to be called. The rest of us anxiously held our breath as other names were added. Finally Mr. Matteau put down his clipboard. Anita, Petou, and I couldn't believe it. We were not on the team.

Marcel pointed to us and said, "They're good players."

Mr. Matteau shook his head. "Girls don't play hockey, Petou is too small, and Danny can't skate."

When I got home, I told Mom what had happened.

"You and Petou and Anita can still have fun playing together," she said. "There will always be games of shinny at the rink."

This didn't make me feel any better. "It's not fair," I said. "We're just as good as the rest!"

Every night was the same. I lay awake staring at the ceiling and talking to myself. "My first chance to wear a uniform and play real hockey, and now it's gone."

Every day after school, I watched from my window as the boys went to the rink. Bingo kept looking at me and wagging his tail. He couldn't understand why we didn't go out to play.

Not making the team was the biggest disappointment of my life.

Weeks later, one snowy Saturday, there was a knock at the door. There stood Mr. Matteau, pointing his finger at me and grinning.

"Danny," he said, "we need you to play goal this afternoon. Tony is hurt. The league has given us special permission to let you play on foot. This is a very important game, you know. If we win, we'll be in the playoffs."

I was so excited, I let out a whoop and jumped back onto Bingo's tail. What a racket!

But even though I was happy, deep down I was afraid. What if I let the team down?

When I got to the rink, all the guys patted me on the back and helped me into Tony's sweater. I was proud, but my heart was pounding.

Marcel whispered, "Don't worry. Just play your game and we'll win."

As I took my position in goal, I saw Anita, Petou, and Bingo watching along the boards. "You can do it, Danny!" they called.

The first period was really rough, with end-to-end action. They scored on me and my spirits dropped, but then we scored twice. The period ended at two to one for the Wolves. I had stopped ten shots out of eleven. I could hardly breathe.

Then, in the second period, they attacked us with all their strength. I stopped twelve shots. But finally a shot went in over my pads. I felt sick. We were tied at two all. I'd let the team down.

The third period was like a bad dream. The shots came at me from all sides. I stopped them with every part of my body. It seemed impossible that we could win.

With only two minutes to go, Marcel rushed up the ice, stick handled through their defence and slipped the puck under their goalie. At the final whistle, we piled on top of each other in a great heap. We had won the game three to two!

Mr. Matteau came onto the ice and put his arms around Marcel and me. "You two saved the game for us," he said. "Danny, I want you to stay on the team. What do you say?"

I spotted Anita and Petou waving in the crowd. Suddenly I knew what I wanted most of all. I looked at Marcel and he nodded. I pointed to my friends and said, "They play the rest of the year with the Wolves, too."

Mr. Matteau laughed, but he promised. Then he took us all to Chong's Café for treats.

Our hearts glowed with the joy of victory. It was a night we would remember all our lives. ◗

●

Find out more about the old days. Ask grown-ups to tell you stories about playing games with their friends when they were young.

Something to Think About

Here are Mr. Matteau's reasons for not choosing Danny and his friends for the team:

- "Girls don't play hockey." (Anita)
- "Petou is too small."
- "Danny can't skate."

Think about each of these reasons. Are they fair or not fair? Pair up with a partner and share your ideas. What other solutions could Mr. Matteau have come up with?

Congratulations! You've completed the story!

Understanding the Story

Instant Replay

- Why did Danny and his friends like winter?

- How did Danny get his nickname? Do you think the name suited him?

- Why were Danny, Anita, and Petou not chosen for the hockey team? How do you think they felt?

- How did Danny get his chance to play, after all?

- Danny had three "best" friends. Is it possible to have more than one best friend? Explain your answer.

- What do you predict will happen to Danny and his friends next hockey season?

Loyalty Web

How did Danny show his loyalty to his friends? Talk about a time when you were loyal to a friend, or a friend was loyal to you. Perhaps you picked her for the baseball team. Perhaps he invited you to a special party. Make a big web in your notebooks or on the chalkboard showing ways of being loyal to a friend.

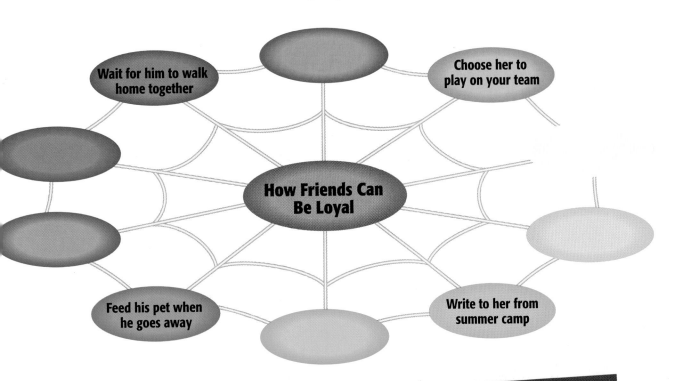

Wait for him to walk home together

Choose her to play on your team

How Friends Can Be Loyal

Feed his pet when he goes away

Write to her from summer camp

Viewing the Illustrations

William Brownridge painted his own pictures to illustrate his story. Look at them again to find

- kids in action
- details about the "old days" on the Prairies
- how the artist contrasts night and day
- the way you can almost "see" the cold

Read more about William Brownridge on page 20.

The Moccasin Goalie

William Roy Brownridge

by Catherine Rondina

It was a great day when the local hockey team made it to the finals, and the coach asked young William Brownridge to play goal in a playoff game. William was thrilled! The league gave special permission to allow him to play in his moccasins. To top it off, the team, the Vawn Cougars, won the championship.

This is the true story that became the picture book, *The Moccasin Goalie.* William Brownridge wrote the story and painted the pictures that illustrate it.

"I carried the story around in my head for years," William says. *"The Moccasin Goalie* is about me and my friends, but it's also about being different. The story shows that being different doesn't mean you can't succeed."

Boyhood on the Prairies

William Brownridge was born in Rosetown, Saskatchewan, the youngest of five children. The doctor noticed right away that there was something wrong with his legs. Both feet were misshapen, so the doctor put casts on them. William also had spina bifida, a serious disorder of the spine. When he was one year old, he became very sick from the casts and almost died.

Because of William's problems, his family had to travel often to the big city—Winnipeg, Manitoba—for medical help.

"It was the Depression and people were very poor," William remembers. "But my father was a station agent for the Canadian National Railway, so we were lucky. We could get free train passes to go back and forth to the hospital."

William had happy times, too. He spent many hours at the train station in Vawn, Saskatchewan, where his father worked. He loved watching the trains and the passengers coming and going. To pass the time, he began drawing pictures of what he saw.

William's illness kept him away from school a lot. But when he could he played with his friends in the neighbourhood. He wore leather moccasins, the only shoes that fit his feet. He even wore them when he played hockey.

"I loved hockey," William says. "I would play in the cold for hours. But because I didn't have any feeling in my legs, they often got frostbitten. My dad finally got a loud whistle to call me off the ice when he figured I'd had enough."

Artist and Writer

When William was sixteen, doctors decided to remove one of his legs. He would have to use crutches for the rest of his life. But William didn't let this keep him from his dream—to become an artist. After studying graphic arts, he became a designer in Calgary, Alberta.

Today William has retired from his job, but he has plenty to do. "I keep very busy as an artist and a writer," William explains. "I also visit schools all over Western Canada and talk with the students."

Fans of *The Moccasin Goalie* have something new to cheer about. William has published a second book about the same gang of kids. It's called *The Final Game.*

William Brownridge designed these uniforms for the NHL's Calgary Flames.

FLAMES HOME UNIFORM

FLAMES AWAY UNIFORM

When My Friend Anita Runs

When my friend Anita runs
she runs straight into the headalong—
legs flashing over the grass, daisies, mounds.

When my friend Anita runs
she sticks out her chest like an Olympic
champion—face all serious concentration.

And you'll never catch her looking around,
until she flies into the invisible tape
that says, she's won.

Then she turns to give me
this big grin and hug.

O to be able to run like Anita,
    run like Anita,
Who runs like a cheetah.
If only, just for once, I could beat her.

Poem by
Grace Nichols

Picture by
Dušan Petričić

Personal Response

- Would you like to have Anita as a friend? Why, or why not?
- What lines in the poem did you like best? Why?

Understanding the Poem

Race to the Finish Line

On your mark *verses one to three:*

The poet paints a picture of Anita racing over the fields and flying into the "invisible tape"—can you see it?

- Do you think Anita's friend admires her? Why?

Get set *verse four:*

Anita turns and hugs her friend.

- How does Anita feel about winning the race? How do you know?

GO! *verse five:*

You reach the real finish line—the last line of the poem.

- What do you discover about the friend's true feelings? Have you ever had a similar feeling? Tell about it.

Read Like a Writer

Similes

Grace Nichols writes that Anita "runs like a cheetah." What does she mean? Here are some more animal comparisons, or similes. With a partner, talk about what each means.

- Radica runs like a deer.
- Amral eats like a horse.
- Andrew is as clumsy as a bull in a china shop.

Think of other animal similes to share with the class. Then plan to use a simile next time you write a poem or a story.

The Southpaw

Story by
Judith Viorst

Pictures by
Ron Tanaka

Dear Richard,
Don't invite me to your birthday party because I'm not coming. And give back the Disneyland sweatshirt I said you could wear. If I'm not good enough to play on your team, I'm not good enough to be friends with.
Your former friend,
Janet
P.S. I hope when you go to the dentist he finds 20 cavities.

BEFORE READING

Here's a different kind of story—a letter story. Richard and Janet write notes and letters to each other. Read the story to find out why they are so angry with each other.

WILLIE MAYS OF

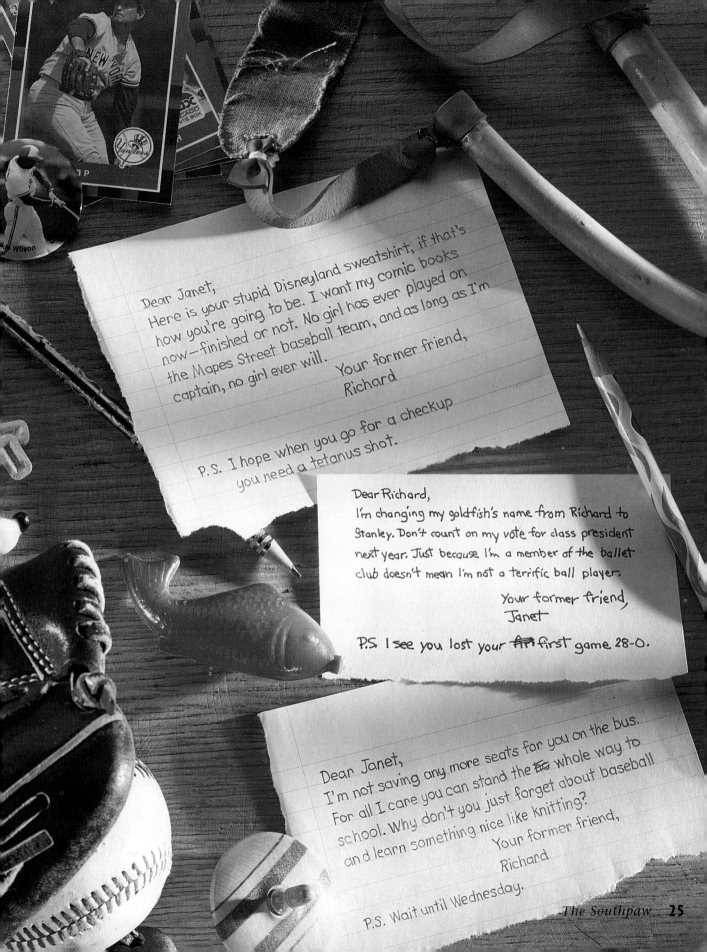

Dear Janet,
Here is your stupid Disneyland sweatshirt, if that's
how you're going to be. I want my comic books
now—finished or not. No girl has ever played on
the Mapes Street baseball team, and as long as I'm
captain, no girl ever will.

Your former friend,
Richard

P.S. I hope when you go for a checkup
you need a tetanus shot.

Dear Richard,
I'm changing my goldfish's name from Richard to
Stanley. Don't count on my vote for class president
next year. Just because I'm a member of the ballet
club doesn't mean I'm not a terrific ball player.

Your former friend,
Janet

P.S. I see you lost your ~~fri~~ first game 28-0.

Dear Janet,
I'm not saving any more seats for you on the bus.
For all I care you can stand the ~~ES~~ whole way to
school. Why don't you just forget about baseball
and learn something nice like knitting?

Your former friend,
Richard

P.S. Wait until Wednesday.

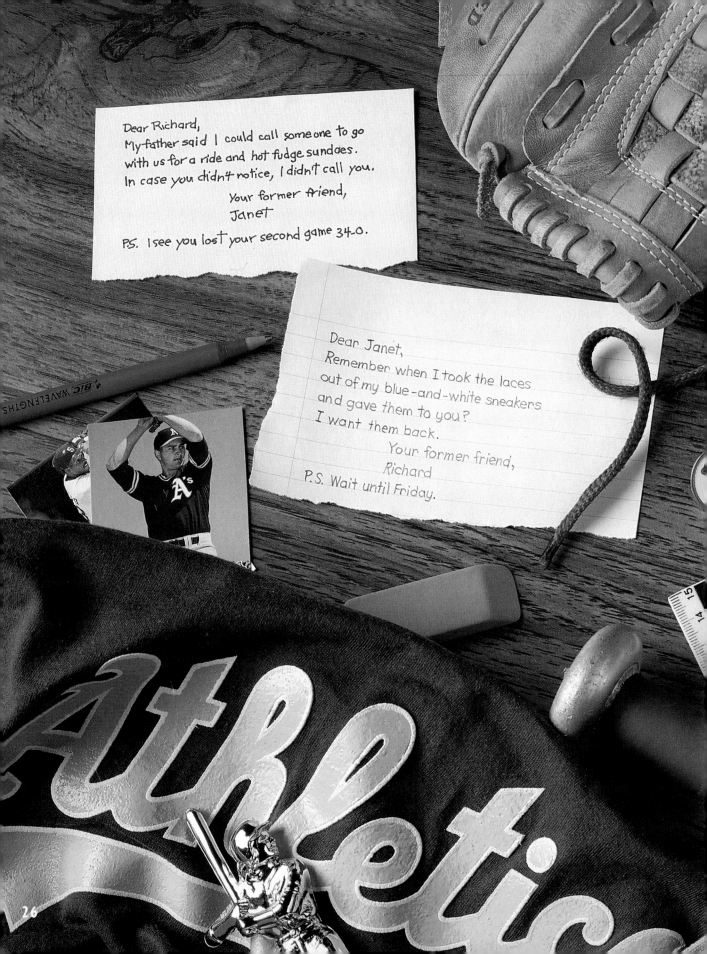

Dear Richard,
My father said I could call some one to go with us for a ride and hot fudge sundaes. In case you didn't notice, I didn't call you.
Your former friend,
Janet
P.S. I see you lost your second game 34-0.

Dear Janet,
Remember when I took the laces out of my blue-and-white sneakers and gave them to you? I want them back.
Your former friend,
Richard
P.S. Wait until Friday.

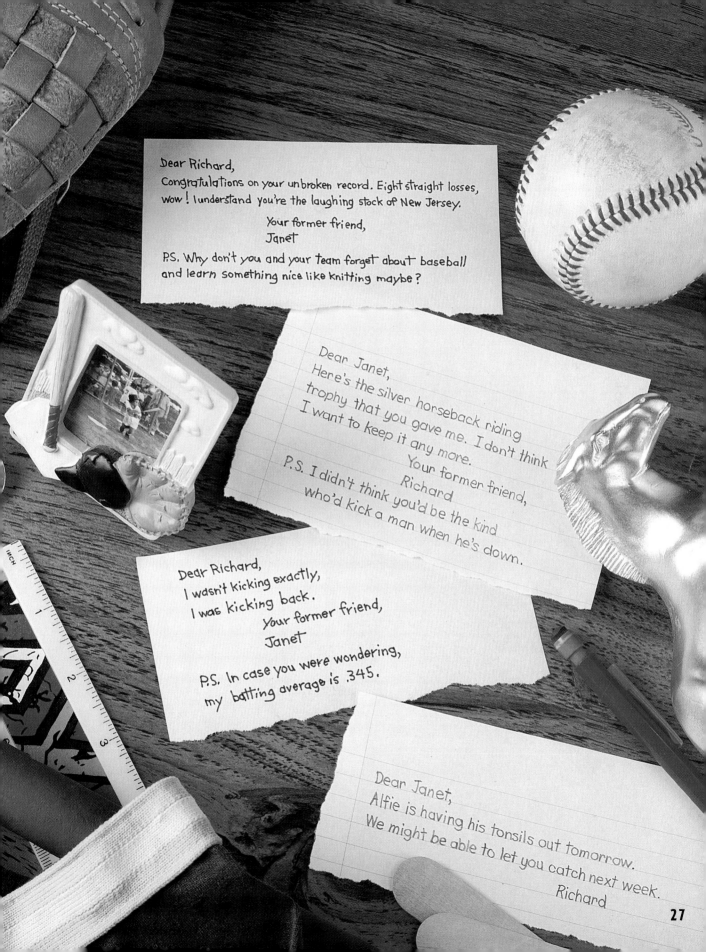

Dear Richard,
Congratulations on your unbroken record. Eight straight losses,
wow! I understand you're the laughing stock of New Jersey.

Your former friend,
Janet

P.S. Why don't you and your team forget about baseball
and learn something nice like knitting maybe?

Dear Janet,
Here's the silver horseback riding
trophy that you gave me. I don't think
I want to keep it any more.
Your former friend,
Richard
P.S. I didn't think you'd be the kind
who'd kick a man when he's down.

Dear Richard,
I wasn't kicking exactly,
I was kicking back.
Your former friend,
Janet

P.S. In case you were wondering,
my batting average is .345.

Dear Janet,
Alfie is having his tonsils out tomorrow.
We might be able to let you catch next week.
Richard

27

Dear Janet,
    PLEASE!
    NOT MARILYN JACKSON.

        Richard

Dear Richard,
Nobody ever said that I was
unreasonable. How about Lizzie
Martindale instead?
                Janet

Dear Janet,
At least could you call your
goldfish Richard again?
            Your friend,
            Richard

29

Understanding the Story

Go for a Home Run

This is a story about two friends who are having a big fight. But instead of yelling at each other, they write letters.

FIRST BASE What are Richard and Janet fighting about?

SECOND BASE How do Janet and Richard try to resolve the conflict?

THIRD BASE How would you try to resolve the conflict?

HOME RUN Who wins in the end? How?

Remember to support your answers with details from the story.

Prepare a Dramatic Reading

You and a partner can have fun reading *The Southpaw* aloud. Who will play the role of Richard? Who will be Janet? First read the letters silently to be sure you understand them very well. Pay close attention to the punctuation marks, too. Then rehearse your oral reading.

If you like, perform *The Southpaw* for the class.

TIPS To make your reading dramatic, you could
- sit at separate desks or chairs, far apart
- pretend you're writing or typing while you speak
- wear a baseball cap or T-shirt

Congratulations! You've made the reading team!

How Not to Resolve a Conflict

Here are some adjectives that describe Janet's and Richard's behaviour. Choose words from the box to fill the blanks in the following sentences.

Adjectives

angry	bragging	immature
stubborn	insulting	pleading

When Janet

...asked for her sweatshirt back, she was _____.

...told Richard her batting average was .345, she was _____.

...refused to play any position but pitcher, she was _____.

When Richard

...said no girl would ever play on his team, he was _____.

...told Janet to take up knitting, he was _____.

...begged Janet to rename her goldfish "Richard," he was _____.

YOUR TURN TO WRITE

A Letter Story

Here are the elements of a friendly letter:

Think of a story you could tell by writing letters. Choose two characters (like Richard and Janet), and get them writing short letters to each other. If you have a key pal, ask her to help you write the letters. Have fun!

Your address
360 Maple Drive
Saskatoon, SK
S6W P3R

The date
April 1, 2001

Your friend's address
4 Snowy Lane
Whitehorse, YT
R2D 2U4

The salutation
Dear Ricky,

The body
Thank you for the birthday card. I loved the joke. At least, I think it was a joke...

The closing
Cheers,
Aaron

Poem by **Beverly McLoughland**
Pictures by **Margaret Hathaway**

Lisa's father is
Black
And her mother is
White,
And her skin is a
Cinnamon
Delight,
Her hair is
Dark
And her eyes are
Light,
And Lisa is
Lisa,
Day and
Night.

And Lisa is
Lisa,
Night and
Day,
Though there are
People
Who sometimes
Say —

Well, is Lisa
That,
Or is Lisa
This? —
Lisa is
Everything
She is.

Lisa is
Lisa,
Day and
Night,
And her skin is a
Cinnamon
Delight,

And Lisa is
Sun
And Lisa is
Star,
And Lisa is
All
The dreams that
Are.

RESPONDING
to LISA

Personal Connection

Have you ever heard people say, "You look just like your mother"? Or, "She's stubborn, just like her father"? In what ways are you similar to members in your family? How are you different?

Media Link TV Friends

What kinds of friends do you see on television? Complete the chart below using information from your favourite TV shows.

Kinds of Friends	Names of TV Friends	Name of TV Program
best friends		
neighbourhood friends		
family friends		
school friends		

In your opinion, are the friendships you see on television realistic or not? Why?

Something To Think About

There is a wise saying: *Don't judge people by the colour of their skin.*

- **What does the saying mean?**

- **Do you think the poet, Beverly McLoughland, would agree with this saying?**

Understanding the Poem

- How is Lisa similar to her parents? How is she different?

- The poet writes, "Lisa is Lisa, Day and Night." What do you think the poet means?

- What is the message of the poem?

BEFORE READING

In this story, Gita has left her friends and family in India to start a new life in Canada.

As you read the story, think about why Gita feels so unhappy at festival time (Divali).

Words from India

Hindu: (HIN doo) a religion that began in India

Divali: (dee VAH lee) Hindu festival of lights

New Delhi: (New DEL ee) capital city of India

diya: (DEE ya) oil lamp in a small clay pot

perras and **jallebies: (PER ahs, jah LAY bees)** Indian sweets

Lights for Gita

Story by Rachna Gilmore

Pictures by Jackie Besteman

GITA PULLED HER HAT DOWN over her ears as she stepped off the school bus.

"Divali," she whispered. "Today's really and truly Divali."

But nothing in the November gloom seemed like Divali.

Today, New Delhi would be glowing with celebration. All her aunts, uncles, and cousins would be together at her grandparents' house. They'd be laughing, talking, and exchanging sweets with friends and neighbours. In the evening they'd light diyas to honour the Goddess Lakshmi who brought prosperity and happiness. And then—fireworks. The whole city would be brilliant with fireworks.

Gita looked anxiously at the dark clouds.

"Please, please don't rain."

Papa had said, "I'll be home early—with fireworks for our first Divali in our new home."

It wouldn't be like Divali at her grandparents'. Still, Mummy had made their favourite sweets—golden perras, spiral jallebies—and she'd let Gita invite five school friends to help celebrate. Gita had wanted to invite her whole class, but you had to be quiet in an apartment.

Not outside, though. Fireworks, lots of them—that's what Divali was all about, the Festival of Lights.

Gita glared at the grey sky before racing up the creaky stairs to their apartment.

She flung her arms around her mother. Papa was home early, just as he'd promised.

"Did you get the fireworks, Papa?"

"Yes, I got them," he said slowly. "But Gita, Divali isn't just fireworks. There's ... "

"Show me, Papa, where are they?"

Gently, Papa turned Gita toward the window. A large drop splashed against the glass. Then another and another.

"It won't last long," said Gita, her voice wobbly.

"The forecast says freezing rain tonight," said Papa. "Never mind. We'll have the fireworks tomorrow."

"But I promised my friends … "

"We'll turn on all the lights," said Mummy. "And light the diyas. You and your friends will have a lovely party."

Gita blinked back her tears.

"Come," said her mother. "Change into your new dress. Then we'll light the diyas."

Gita and her mother set the little clay pots along the windowsills and around the room. Needles of ice stung the windows. Freezing rain on Divali! How could such a place ever be home?

Last year Divali had been warm and joyful. She and her cousins had startled everyone with noisy crackers called little rascals. They'd whispered in the prayer room as the incense smoke curled upward and the grown-ups chanted. Grandmother had told them stories of Prince Ram and his wife Sita and of their homecoming on Divali. And in the evening! Cones spouted fountains of fire, Catherine wheels whirled, and hissing rockets burst into dazzling showers of colour.

A sudden gust rattled the window. Gita stuck out her tongue. You can't get in! And you won't spoil my party! She gave a hard twist to the wisps of cotton wick.

Mummy, bangles tinkling, filled the diyas with mustard oil. As she finished, the phone rang.

Gita heard the murmur of her mother's voice, the click of the receiver, and then more ringing.

She shook the box of matches impatiently as her mother came back. "Can I light the first one?"

Mummy just smiled and smoothed Gita's hair.

"That was Jennie and Helga. It's too icy to drive, they can't come."

The phone rang again.

Gita ran to her room. She burrowed into bed, and jerked the covers over her head. "I hate this place," she sobbed.

Mummy lifted back the covers and gently hugged Gita.

"Amy hasn't called. And she does live nearby."

Gita pulled away and blew her nose.

"Gita," said Mummy softly. "Divali is really about filling the darkness with light. Fireworks can't do it for us. We must do it ourselves." Mummy's smile was bright, but also sad—like grandmother's smile when they'd said goodbye.

For a long moment Gita sat still. Then she managed a watery smile. "Let's light the diyas."

One by one, golden flames quivered and sprang to life. The warm fragrance of mustard oil filled the room.

Just as Gita lit the last wick the electric lights flickered—on, off, on again. Then all the lights—in the apartment, in all the houses, even the street lamps—died.

Darkness on Divali! Gita's throat tightened.

Then she began to laugh.

In the sudden rush of darkness their diyas glowed—bright, brighter, brightest—filling the living room with light.

"We beat the darkness, we beat the darkness!" Gita clapped her hands.

"Lakshmi will come for sure. We'll have wonderful luck," said Mummy.

Gita ran to the window. The diyas' reflection made it seem as if there were another shining room outside. She sang softly. Drops of freezing rain glittered as they flew past.

Slowly, the headlights of a car came down the street and stopped in front of their building. "It's Amy!" shouted Gita.

Papa started downstairs with the flashlight. Gita ran ahead in the bouncing circle of light. She opened the front door.

"Careful, it's icy," called Papa.

Gita took a few cautious steps. She stopped, eyes wide.

The whole world glistened! The sidewalks, every branch, every twig, the lamppost, even the blades of grass!

In the dark city, only their windows blazed with the steady glow of diyas. The ice, reflecting their light, sparkled and danced like fireworks.

Amy's voice brought her back. "Gita, tomorrow we can go sliding. It'll be like flying."

Gita's eyes shone. She'd have to write her grandparents about this Divali in her new home. "Hey, Amy, let's play hide and seek while the power's still out."

She took one last look at the light singing in the heart of the ice. "Come on," she shouted, "race you upstairs!" ⬢

FOLLOW UP

• Why was Gita unhappy at Divali time?

• How did Gita's parents try to make her feel better?

Making New Friends

It's not easy to make new friends when you move or go to a new school. In your group, talk about ways you could help a new student to meet people and feel more at home. Share your ideas with the class.

You're in the "**Good Reading**" Spotlight

What Is Divali?

Divali, a Festival of Lights which falls in October or November, is observed by Hindus all over the world. It is a magical family time that honours Lakshmi, the Goddess of Wealth who brings good fortune and prosperity to all throughout the year. It also celebrates the homecoming of Prince Ram and his wife Sita, as told in the Hindu epic *Ramayana*. Lots of sweets, parties, storytelling, and fireworks make this a holiday particularly loved by children.

Understanding the Story

Lighting the Diyas

• How are Gita's party plans spoiled?

• What does Gita mean when she laughs and says, "We beat the darkness!"?

• When Gita rushes out to meet Amy, she sees that the city looks beautiful. Why?

• What if you had to move to a new country? What would you be the most excited about? What might you be worried about?

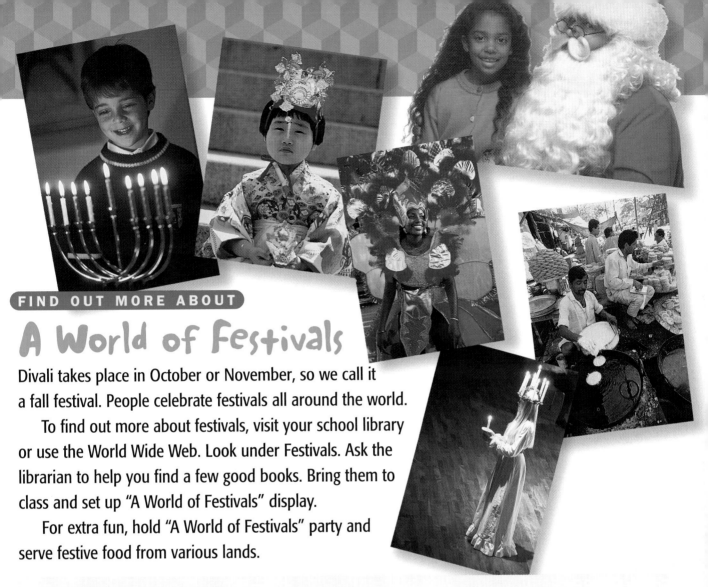

A World of Festivals

Divali takes place in October or November, so we call it a fall festival. People celebrate festivals all around the world.

To find out more about festivals, visit your school library or use the World Wide Web. Look under Festivals. Ask the librarian to help you find a few good books. Bring them to class and set up "A World of Festivals" display.

For extra fun, hold "A World of Festivals" party and serve festive food from various lands.

MORE GOOD READING

The Gift by Joseph Kertes

Jacob was a Jewish boy from Hungary. More than anything, he longed to celebrate the holidays with his new Canadian friends. This funny-sad story tells what happened when he finally got his wish. (a short story book)

A Friend Like Zilla by Rachna Gilmore

Zenobia's vacation in Prince Edward Island is going well. She's having tons of fun with Zilla, the girl from the next-door farm, feeding seagulls and such. But trouble arrives with Uncle Chad, who just can't understand how Zilla can be 17 years old. (a chapter book)

The Dragon's Egg by Alison Baird

Ai Lien is lonely at her new school. What's worse, the bully, Jake Bradley, won't stop picking on her. What a surprise, then, when her best friend and protector hatches out of a dragon's egg from China! (a chapter book)

Animals &Us

My Olympic Tabby Cat

Poem by **Lola Sneyd**
Picture by **Marion Stuck**

Dancing leaves invite you
Lightly you bounce
down the wooden steps
Paw-bat the wind-tossed
golden birch and bronze oak leaves
Race around the old oak tree
Faster
Faster
The leaves dance higher
You leap and dance
Higher
Higher

A dry oak leaf catches
against the wooden fence

You pounce

Proudly you carry
your bronze medal to me

And race
to capture
a gold

Personal Connection

Think of your cat or a cat you know. What games does your cat play? What is the funniest playful thing your cat friend has done? Tell a story about your cat. You may wish to use multimedia presentation software to help you tell your story.

YOUR TURN TO WRITE

Write a Poem

Lola Sneyd's tabby cat is playing in the Autumn Olympic Games. What "sports" could a cat play in other seasons—the Spring, Summer, or Winter Olympics? What could the "medals" be instead of leaves?

Pick the season you like best and write your own poem about an Olympic pet.

Understanding the Poem

Go for the Gold!

For the Bronze

Q Olympic athletes compete for three types of medals. What are they?

For the Silver

Q What movements does the cat make? What real Olympic events do they remind you of?

For the Gold

Q What do you predict the cat will receive the gold medal for?

"Dancing leaves invite you."

"Lightly you bounce."

Read It Aloud

You can do this activity alone or with a partner.

Poems sound great when you read them aloud, but it takes a little practice. Read *My Olympic Tabby Cat* silently, and think about how you could bring it alive with your voice. Consider

 TIPS

- how people sound when they talk to their cats
- how you can use your voice loudly or softly for contrast
- whether the lines should go slower or faster
- when you might want to pause
- sound effects you might want to use

When you are happy with the way the poem sounds, read it aloud for the class.

What types of pets can you think of?

Make a list in your notebook or on the chalkboard.

Give your list the title "Animal Friends."

Article by Sara Corbett

ANIMALS Make *Good* FRIENDS

Do you have a pet? If you do, you probably think of your pet as one of your best friends. Pets can be important members of a family, needing the same love, care, and respect that people do. In parts of Europe, people can bring their dogs to restaurants with them. Some restaurants even have special pet menus, so you can order your dog a meal to eat right at the table with you!

◀ **Ancient Egyptian statue**
Cats were first domesticated as pets by the ancient Egyptians, and were considered sacred.

Three-toed sloth, Panama ▶
The three-toed sloth is a mammal native to the tropical rain forests of South America.

Baby camel, Niger ▲

People have had pets since prehistoric days. About 15 000 years ago, the first dogs were tamed to live in hunting villages. The cat has been a popular pet since the days of ancient Egypt, when cats were so sacred that if one died, it was mummified and buried in a special cat cemetery.

Alpaca, Peru ▶

◀ **Pet bird, Morocco**

49

Dog mosaic, ancient Rome

Romans who had dogs were required to keep a mosaic picture like this one with the words "Beware the dog"(in Latin, "*Cave canem*") outside their homes. ▼

Tarantula, United States ▶

These hairy spiders are commonly found in the southwestern United States. Only the bite of some South American tarantulas may be serious.

Today, if you visit a pet shop or animal breeder in your neighbourhood, you're likely to see animals that originally came from different parts of the world. The iguana, the cockatoo, and the guinea pig, for example, are animals native to South America that are kept as pets all over the world.

We now know enough about these different kinds of animals and how they breed. We can provide them with the right temperature, food, and setting to live comfortably, even in a place that's thousands of kilometres away from their native land. Unfortunately, some exotic animals, like tropical birds and monkeys, are captured and sold illegally as pets.

In certain parts of the world, you'll find people with pets from the surrounding environment. These types of pets can give you clues to their natural habitat. For example, in the warm, forested regions of Madagascar, the tree-dwelling chameleon is a popular pet. In Alaska and northern Canada, big furry dogs like the Malamute are good pets because they can withstand very cold temperatures.

Chameleon, Madagascar ▲
This curious little reptile is famous for changing colours, from green to brown, depending on the temperature of the air.

◄

Malamute puppy, Tuktoyaktuk, Canada
These dogs are treated as family pets when they are pups. As soon as they are big enough to wear a harness, they are trained to work in dog teams.

▶
Armadillos, Mexico
Often, people domesticate animals that live in the surrounding environment. Armadillos, which live in dry, desert regions, are kept as pets in parts of Mexico and other Latin American countries.

51

FOLLOW UP

Which pets in the article were new to you?

Add the new pet names to your list of **"Animal Friends."**

Personal Response

• Which pet in the article interested you the most?

• Which one would you most like to have?

• Which one would you absolutely NOT want? Explain why.

• In your opinion, should exotic animals be kept as pets? Why, or why not?

Animal Categories

Birds	Reptiles	Mammals	Insects
blue jay	snake	horse	mosquito

This chart shows four important categories of animals with an example for each one.

All of the animal friends in the article fit into one of these categories. Work together in a small group. Using information in the article, place the animal names on the chart. You may wish to use a database to help you organize your work. If you still don't know where an animal belongs, try

• a dictionary

• a library book about animals

• an encyclopedia (book or CD-ROM)

People have many other kinds of pets and animal friends. Find out about them and add their names to the chart. (You may need new categories like Fish.) If you have Internet access, subscribe to a newsgroup on pets to help you with your research.

YOUR TURN TO WRITE

A Paragraph

Write a paragraph or two about

• **Why My Pet Is My Best Friend**

        or

• **The Pet I Wish For**

Remember that paragraphs

• **are indented**

• **have one main idea**

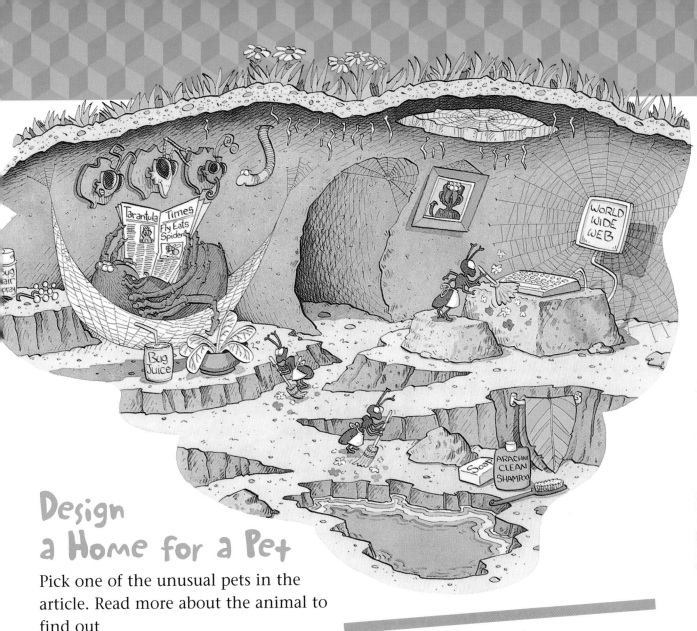

Design a Home for a Pet

Pick one of the unusual pets in the article. Read more about the animal to find out

- what it likes to eat
- what it likes to do
- where it likes to live—indoors or outside, hot or cold place, wet or dry place

Now design a home for your pet where it would be safe and happy. (Cage? house? aquarium? stable? fenced-in field?)

Turn your design into a drawing, a mural, or a model and display it in class.

Words About Animal Homes

habitat: the kind of place where an animal lives (ocean, forest, prairie, etc.)

environment: the combination of habitat, temperature, and food supply that an animal needs to live (rain forest, northern snow and ice, hot dry desert, etc.)

native to: the particular place an animal comes from (Canada, China, Australia, etc.)

domesticate: turn a wild animal into a pet or farm animal that can live with humans

BEFORE READING

When Craig notices that Stripey is missing, he knows he'll have to find her. But nobody has time to go searching for a Husky puppy with him. Read the story to find out

- how Craig follows clues in the forest

- who his surprise helper is

Story by
Diana C. Conway

Pictures by
Luc Melanson

Hunting WITH Raven

Craig counts the puppies again to make sure. One, two, three, four fat rear ends stick up from the pan of fish scraps he's just set down. One pup is missing, and it's all Craig's fault. Yesterday he noticed the puppies scratching at the base of the chicken wire fence. He should have carried beach stones up right away to fill the gap. Instead, he stuck a ragged piece of plywood against the fence and hurried off to search for rabbits in the alder bush. He's let Papa down.

Before Papa left for his summer job fighting forest fires, he said, "Craig, you're nine now. Big enough for important work. Since Grandpa's lost his seeing, it's time for you to be the family dog man. You watch the pups at fish camp."

Every summer Mama motors the family down the Yukon River for fish camp. Like other Athabascans,* they net hundreds of upstream-swimming salmon for themselves and their dogs.

Craig bangs the metal pail with a stick. "Come, Stripey. Good dog." Two ravens fly low overhead, brought by the smell of food. But no black husky comes tail-wiggling home. Craig walks slowly around the pen in ever-widening circles, scanning the ground like a hunter, looking for a sign to show whether his puppy has gone upstream or down.

Downstream, big brother Duane has just emptied the fish net. Craig runs to the beached wooden skiff. The boat thumps like a drum from the beating of salmon tails on the floorboards.

"I lost a dog," says Craig.

"Which one?"

"Stripey. With the silver line down her back. Grandpa felt her legs and said she'll be the best sled dog of the litter."

Duane says, "Too bad. Not much chance she'll survive alone in the woods. Lots of bears hanging around on account of the salmon."

"Help me look for her?"

"Can't." Duane slaps a mosquito on Craig's shoulder, leaving a fish-slime hand print on the red flannel shirt. "Like to, but I've got to gut these fish right away."

---

* Many First Nations people living in Alaska, the Yukon, and across northwestern Canada speak **Athabascan** languages. Examples are the Kutchin, the Tutchone, and the Dogrib peoples.

Craig carries one of the fish to the table where Mama and big sister Brenda are preparing the salmon for smoking. The sun flashes on their half moon knives as they slice fillets to hang over wooden racks.

"Mama, I'm going to look in the woods for Stripey."

"Only as far as the stream, Craig. Don't want to lose you, too."

Brenda hands him a chunk of warm smoked salmon on a paper plate. "For strength," she says.

"Make noise to warn off the bears," calls Duane.

"And don't stay too long." Mama's worried frown pulls her blue bandana down a little over her forehead.

Craig runs down the path toward the woods. He slows to tiptoe past the white canvas tent where Grandpa sits listening to the river. Grandpa mustn't know he's been careless with the dogs. He sneaks past without cracking a stick, but Grandpa calls out, "Where you go, boy?"

"How'd you know it was me, Grandpa?"

"Eyes no good, make me hear better." English is hard for Grandpa. He speaks to Papa and Mama in Athabascan. "Smell fish, too."

Craig laughs. He hands Grandpa the plate. "Have some."

They share the smoked salmon while Craig tells about Stripey. "What if a bear gets her, Grandpa? Oh, I just wish you could help me look."

"Watch Raven, little hunter."

"What, Grandpa?"

But that's all the old man says by way of goodbye.

Craig walks between the alder bushes, searching for a footprint pressed in mud or a clump of dog hair on a branch. Rabbit droppings litter the ground, but there's no sign of Stripey. Beyond the alders, the birch forest begins. The ground is a puzzle of sun and leaf shadows. Craig feels the eyes of hidden animals on him as he walks.

He whistles and calls, "Come, Stripey. Come and eat." Once he thinks he hears her yip beyond a bend. It's only a chattering squirrel. Craig rests, panting, and swats at a thick cloud of mosquitoes around his face. Maybe Stripey is already dead, torn to pieces by a bear or a wolverine. Perhaps he'll never again feel her warm tongue wash his cheek or her furry tail beat his shins.

Craig stares at the ground. Through the water that stings his eyes he notices a small clump of soft belly hair snagged on a wild rosebush. Carefully, he moves forward, searching for more signs. Fifteen minutes later he finds a damp spot on the leaves where a dog has squatted. His heart is like a butterfly inside him, but it seems to skip a beat when he reaches the stream where Mama told him to turn back.

Surely Stripey is near, even though she doesn't answer his calls. He has to search a little farther, no matter what Mama said. Last year, before Grandpa lost his seeing completely, they climbed together down the steep banks of the stream. He's big enough now to find his way alone. The sun is sinking low, but in July this far north there's some light all night long.

A harsh cry splits the air. "Gga gga!" cries Raven, the sacred bird of the Athabascans.

"Watch Raven," Grandpa said. Craig remembers now that Raven's cry means "animal" in the Athabascan language. Sometimes Raven shows hunters where game is hidden. The big, black bird circles gracefully on the far side of the stream. Maybe Raven is showing him where Stripey lies scared or hurt. Of course, Raven is a trickster who doesn't always tell the truth. What if he's only trying to make Craig get lost far from camp?

Craig weighs Mama's words against Grandpa's, looking for a way to satisfy them both. Then he takes off his red flannel shirt and ties it to a tree branch. From the other side he'll be able to see the path home again. One step at a time he finds his way down the rocky slope and across the shallow stream. He claws his way up the other side, grabbing at roots for a handhold.

When he reaches the top, Craig looks around for Raven. The trickster is nowhere to be seen. In the bushes to the left, a crunch of dried leaves makes Craig gasp. Has Raven led him to a bear? Shivers work their way from his belly to the top of his head like a million crawling ants. Something round and black moves through the brush. Craig raises his hands high to make himself look bigger and calls, "Hey, bear. Watch out for me."

The animal waddles out from the bushes, and Craig bursts out laughing. It's only a fat porcupine. Craig wipes his sweaty palms on his jeans and holds perfectly still, closing his eyes to hear the way Grandpa hears. Over the buzz of mosquitoes and the trickle of the stream, he catches a low, whimpering sound. And then Raven calls again, "Gga gga." Craig opens his eyes. He bounds to where the bird is circling. Stripey lies next to a currant bush, her paw trapped in a wire noose set to catch rabbits. She barks him a welcome.

"Poor girl," Craig says. He reaches down and releases the snare. Stripey jumps hard against his chest, knocking him over. She licks the happy tears from his face. He examines her leg carefully. The fine wire has gashed the black fur but not cut badly into the muscle. Grandpa will know how to cure her.

Craig remembers that Raven has helped him. "Thank you, Old Grandfather," he calls out respectfully. He sights his red shirt on the opposite bank and heads for the home path. Stripey bounces at his feet, showing only the barest limp. Craig hopes that, come fall, Papa will let him help train her to pull the dogsled. ◆

Choose a partner. Discuss what you found out about

- the clues Craig followed
- his surprise helper

Understanding the Story

Raven's Tricks

- During the summer, everyone in Craig's family has a job to do. What do each of these people do?

Papa	**Craig**	**Duane**
Mama	**Brenda**	**Grandpa**

- What makes Stripey a very special puppy?
- Why can't Craig be sure that Raven will help him to find Stripey?
- Do you think Stripey's foot will get better? How do you know?
- Do you think *Hunting with Raven* is a good title for the story? Explain your answer.

FIND OUT MORE ABOUT

Sled Dogs

Imagine that you are helping train Stripey to pull a dogsled. You need to find out more about sled dogs and how to train them. Look for books at the library, check out some CD-ROMs, and maybe search the Internet. Look for answers to some of these and other questions:

- What do sled dogs eat?
- Are they pets, or working animals, or both?
- How do they learn to pull the sled?
- How does the lead dog control the team?

Congratulations! You found your way through the story!

Turn a Story into a TV Show

Imagine that you are a television director. You think that *Hunting with Raven* would make a great TV show. Now you need to convince a TV producer to make the show. Here are some ideas:

- Tell the producer the story by writing one or two paragraphs.
- Explain who the audience would be for the show.
- Give some interesting facts about sled dogs.

- Describe how you would show Raven, the trickster, on television.
- Suggest a few actors who would be good in the roles.

Use your own drawings, or pictures cut out of magazines, to make your presentation exciting!

RAVEN PRODUCTIONS
T.V. SHOW PROPOSAL FOR
"Hunting With Raven"

The Story

The Audience

Actors

Interesting Facts

Raven

3 Poems

by
X. J. Kennedy

Pictures by
Philippe Beha

The Earthworm

Said an earthworm to me, "Beg your pardon,
May I bore a few holes in your garden?
It may seem to you odd
That I'd chew through a clod,
But I don't want our planet to harden."

The Shark

Said the mom of the baby blue shark,
"Try that beach at the national park.
You'll have wonderful fun
Making everyone run—
Just be sure, dear, you're home before dark."

The Whales off Wales

With walloping tails, the whales off Wales
Whack waves to wicked whitecaps.
And while they snore on their watery floor,
They wear wet woollen nightcaps.

The whales! the whales! the whales off Wales,
They're always spouting fountains.
And as they glide through the tilting tide,
They move like melting mountains.

Write A Poem

- Which poem did you find the funniest?

- Write your own funny poem about an animal. Imitate the pattern of one of X.J. Kennedy's poems, or make up your own.

In this article, you will find out about four endangered animals and birds. After you read about each one, make notes under these headings:

- **Habitat**

- **Food**

- **Why It is Endangered**

POEMS AND TEXT BY
Colleayn O. Mastin

PICTURES BY
Jan Sovak

CANADIAN ENDANGERED SPECIES

Cougar

The mountain lion or cougar,
Is a sly and stealthy cat,
It truly is carnivorous,
Eats moose and things like that.

This solitary hunter
Is very hard to see,
As it creeps through
* mountain forests,*
As hungry as can be.

The cougar is the largest cat in Canada. This fierce cat is endangered in the eastern parts of Canada, but seems to be surviving quite well in the mountains of Alberta and British Columbia.

Cougar skin and meat have little value, but a cougar pelt is often used as a trophy-rug or wall hanging. Hunting, trapping, poisonings, and the taking over of its habitat by people are reasons that it is endangered. Other than humans, the cougar's only enemy is the wolf.

Cougars prefer to eat deer, but beaver, rabbits, birds, and even mice and frogs are also hunted for food. They sometimes attack cattle.

In midsummer, female cougars give birth to two or three kittens. They are raised only by the mother, and they stay with her for a year.

Black-Footed Ferret

Near the burrows of the prairie dog
The black-footed ferret once thrived;
Where prairie dogs set up a "town,"
The black-footed ferret arrived.

But prairie dog's homes grew fewer,
When their grasslands were taken away;
Then the black-footed ferret discovered
That it had no place to stay.

Before people came to the Prairies, there were thousands of small, brown, burrowing prairie dogs, the favourite food of the black-footed ferret. When the prairie dogs seemed to be eating too much of the farmers' grass, they were killed by poisoning and hunting.

This led to the disappearance of the ferret. For as well as eating prairie dogs, these ferrets would often take over their burrows and make their homes in the middle of a prairie dog town.

Before ferrets became a seriously endangered species, the female would give birth to three to five young ones in late spring.

Today, the black-footed ferret is described as "the rarest North American mammal."

Whooping Crane

The tallest bird in Canada
Is called the whooping crane;
Where once it had its breeding grounds,
There now are fields of grain.

These beautiful great fliers
Have wings two metres wide;
They soar aloft on rising air,
Then elegantly glide.

Each winter, whooping cranes make a long and dangerous flight from northern Canada to Texas. Then, in April they return to their northern nesting grounds. Here the female lays two eggs in a large nest made of bulrushes. Usually, only one of the two chicks that hatch survives.

To increase the survival rate of the chicks, naturalists have used sandhill cranes as "foster parents." They remove an egg from a whooping crane's nest and place it in a sandhill crane's nest, where it will have a better chance to hatch as a healthy chick.

At one time, there were only fifteen whooping cranes alive. Now there are more than two hundred. It is against the law to harm a whooping crane.

CANADIAN ENDANGERED SPECIES

Spotted Owl

To see a spotted owl
Is a sight that's very rare;
In the mountains of the west coast,
They are down to a few pair.

They live in old growth forests
Fly at night, but not by day,
When human beings disturb them,
These owls move away.

CANADIAN
ENDANGERED
SPECIES

Normally, spotted owls stay close to home all the year-round. But when the old growth forests where they live are threatened by roads and logging, they have to find a safer place to build new nests.

Spotted owls hunt only at night, feeding on squirrels and other small rodents. They have very large black eyes which allow them to see in the dark. When they hoot, it sounds something like the barking of a dog.

In a nest high up in a tall coniferous tree, the females of this rare species lay two or three plain white eggs. These owls are still in danger of extinction. The spotted owl population in Canada is probably no more than fifteen pairs.

RESPONDING

to CANADIAN ENDANGERED SPECIES

FOLLOW UP

Use the notes you made to complete the activity, **Make a Chart**.

Complete the following chart using information in the article.

Make a Chart

	HABITAT	FOOD	WHY IT IS ENDANGERED
Black-Footed Ferret			
Cougar			
Whooping Crane			
Spotted Owl			

Good work!
You have just found out a lot about endangered animals and birds.

When you've finished, check your chart with a partner and see if you can agree on all the facts. (That's what scientists do.)

Important Words

threatened: a species that may soon become endangered

endangered: a species that is almost extinct, because there are only a few birds or animals left

extinct: a species that no longer exists

Understanding the Article

Species in Danger

- Which of the birds or animals in the article is your favourite? Why?
- People try to help endangered species. How are scientists helping to save the whooping crane?
- Choose one of the other birds or animals in the article. What would you do to help it survive?

If you want to
save endangered
animals and birds, it helps to make sure lots of people know about the problem.
One way is to make and wear a button for your favourite species. Here's how.

Materials: cardboard, scissors, glue, magazines, safety pin

Directions:

1 Cut out a circle or square of cardboard about 5 cm in diameter.

2 Draw a picture of your bird or animal's head, or cut out a photograph in a magazine (about 3 cm in diameter).

3 Paste the picture onto your button.

4 Write a short caption around the picture.

5 Tape a safety pin to the back so you can wear your button.

Wear your button at recess and talk to other students about your endangered species.
As well as designing your button, what other ways can you think of to make people aware of your endangered species?

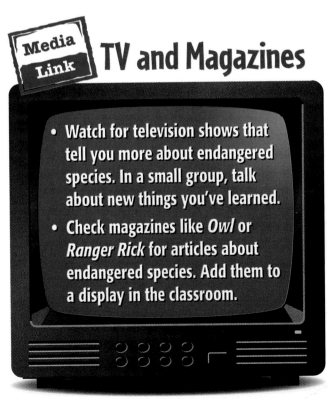

Media Link **TV and Magazines**

- Watch for television shows that tell you more about endangered species. In a small group, talk about new things you've learned.

- Check magazines like *Owl* or *Ranger Rick* for articles about endangered species. Add them to a display in the classroom.

Wolf Watcher

Article by Sami Antaki and Jenny Ryon

Look over this article before you read it. What do you see that helps you predict what the article tells about wolves?

*H*i. I'm Jenny Ryon. That's me in the picture (*below*) with that big, brown wolf. His name's Tracker and I've known him for nearly 12 years.

Tracker's just one of 15 wolves I look after at a place called the Canadian Centre for Wolf Research. That's a large, natural compound in the middle of a Nova Scotia forest. The centre is the perfect place for scientists from all over the world to come and study how wild wolves live. We also get a lot of photographers and filmmakers here.

The Centre has four special places that people use to watch the wolves interact with each other without bothering them.

These places are called observation points. Two of them are log huts and two are trailers. We even have a video camera and tape recorder set up inside one of the wolf dens. That way we can watch how a wolf gives birth and what the pups do once they're born.

Some of the wolves here, like Tracker, have been taken care of by humans their whole lives. But they're still wild animals, and they have to be treated with a lot of respect and care.

> **They make their own rules, choose their own leaders, and take care of themselves.**

I'm lucky because these wolves are used to me now. They let me watch them without being afraid of me. This means the behaviour I see is natural. I've learned how to understand what they're saying with their bodies and their voices.

The other wolves live in two wild packs. They make their own rules, choose their own leaders, and take care of themselves. Sometimes they fight to see who's the strongest. That can be a bit scary to watch.

I feed the wolves once a day. I go to a special spot in the compound and set out a kibbled dog food. From time to

time I drop off a deer that's been killed by a car (*see above*). The wolves eat standing side by side. Sometimes they growl and snap, but they seldom hurt each other. The stronger ones may drive other pack members away, but these guys will come back later and in the end they'll all get to eat as much as they want.

Wolves are really very kind and helpful to each other. I want to tell you what goes on from the time a female is ready to give birth to the time the pups take their place in the pack.

Before Birth

About a week before giving birth a wolf will decide she'd better prepare her den. That's the hole she digs in the side of a hill that will be her home for the next two months. Sometimes she chooses a den that's already been used and just cleans it up.

WOLF FACTS

Wolves are some of the best parents in the animal world. Everyone gets in on raising the pups – aunts and uncles, older brothers and sisters, as well as mother and father.

If she's digging a new den, she doesn't have to do this job alone. Many of the other wolves in the pack—both male and female—come by to help. I've seen them standing in line, waiting for their turn to dig, dig, dig. They'll squeeze into the hole, one by one, until all that's sticking out is their tail. When they start digging the dirt comes flying out between their legs. They look like they're really having fun.

> *I've seen them standing in line, waiting for their turn to dig, dig, dig.*

In the days just before the pups are born the mother stays very close to the den. She won't even go looking for food. Of course, she doesn't starve. Her mate brings her things to eat, and sometimes other wolves in the pack bring her food, too. She's constantly fed, until she's given birth and finished nursing the pups.

Meeting the Family

The birth of the pups is a time for all the wolves in the pack to celebrate. They stand at the den entrance (*see below*) making squeaking noises and wagging their tails. The male wolves try their best to help. One of the funniest things I've seen was when Cuchulain, a yearling male, tried to feed a pup a whole deer leg. It was bigger than the pup! A pup will nuzzle an adult's mouth to let the older wolf know that it's hungry.

Leaving Home

It takes the pups a while to get up the courage to leave their snug home. Maybe that's because they're born blind and deaf (*see page 79*). After about two weeks, though, they're ready to peek their heads out of the den. Slowly, slowly, slowly they venture further and further out.

By the time they're five weeks old they spend most of their day outside the den, playing with all the other wolves in the pack. The big males are very gentle with these small fry. I think they act like favourite uncles. They don't just play with the pups, they feed and groom them, too.

Wolves use many different sounds when they communicate with each other – howls, barks, growls, and yelps. Sometimes pack members squeak at each other in a friendly way.

It's super important for the pups to play. Running, tumbling, and wrestling gives them plenty of exercise. It also teaches them how to communicate with each other. They learn by doing, just as human babies do. By playing with the other members of the pack they learn how to behave, how to start a game with another wolf, and how to keep it going.

Adults and yearlings play pretty rough with each other. If one of them

They learn by doing, just as human babies do.

wants to play with a pup, they have to learn to be gentle or the pup will refuse to join in.

I've been very lucky to have spent so much time near these wonderful animals. Not too many people get that chance. But if more people took the time to understand how a wolf pack behaves, they wouldn't be so scared of them. After all, people and wolves share the same world.

RESPONDING
to **WOLF WATCHER**

FOLLOW UP

Now that you have read the article, how close were your predictions? What helped you the most?

Media Link

Movie Location

Imagine you are making a movie or a documentary and you want some shots of real live wolves. Here's what you do:

Write a fax or an e-mail letter to the Centre for Wolf Research. Explain what your movie will be about. Describe the kinds of wolf shots you would like to get (adults eating or cubs playing). Ask for permission to come to the Centre with a camera operator sometime soon.

Congratulations! You've completed a serious article about wolves.

Career Tip

Jenny Ryon is a biologist—a scientist who studies animals. If you are interested in doing work like hers, you should

- **get to know a lot about animals now**
- **take science courses in high school**
- **choose biology courses in university**
- **try to get summer jobs working with animals**

FAX

To: Jenny Ryon
From: Norm Tewison
Subject: Wolf Movie

Date: 26 February, 2007

Dear Jenny Ryon

I read about the Canadian Centre for Wolf Research in a magazine article. It sounded really interesting. I am a filmmaker, and I'm making a movie about...

80 ANIMALS & US

Do the wolves at a
research centre
behave the same
way as wolves in
the wilderness?

Observe Like a Scientist

Scientists learn a lot about animals just by watching them.
Watching closely is called "observing." Try learning about
a pet, a farm animal, or a city animal near you.

- Observe your animal closely for a week.

- Watch how your animal
behaves at different
times of day and night.

- Try using binoculars,
a tape recorder,
a camera, or
other equipment.

- Write notes of what
you see.

Things to watch for:

❏ *What does it like to eat? Is it fussy about food?*

❏ *Does it fight with other animals?*

❏ *Does it keep itself clean? How?*

❏ *Can you teach it tricks?*

❏ *When does it sleep?*

❏ *Does it like to play?*

❏ *What does it like to do (or not to do)
with people?*

- End up with a list called Things I Learned
About a Cat (or other animal).

- Write a paragraph called What I Could Do to
Make My Dog (or other animal) Happier.

Viewing the Photographs

Take a close look at the
photographs in the article. What
information do they give you
about wolves? For example:
How do wolves look, compared
with dogs?

How and what do they eat?

Where do they build their
dens?

Poem by **Kit Wright**
Pictures by **Renée Mansfield**

OUR HAMSTER'S LIFE

Our hamster's life:
there's not much
to it,
not much
to it.

He presses his pink nose
to the door of the cage
and decides for the fifty-six
millionth time
that he can't get
through it.

Our hamster's life:
there's not much
to it,
not much
to it.

It's about the most boring
life in the world
if he only
knew it.
He sleeps and drinks and
he eats.
He eats and he drinks and
he sleeps.

He slinks and he dreeps.
He eats.

This process
he repeats.

Our hamster's life:
there's not much
to it,
not much
to it.

You'd think it would drive
him bonkers,
going round and round on
his wheel.
It's certainly driving me
bonkers,

watching him
do it.

But he may be thinking:
"That boy's life,
there's not much
to it,
not much
to it:

watching a hamster go
round on a wheel,
It's driving me bonkers if
he only knew it,

watching him
watching me
do it."

RESPONDING
to OUR HAMSTER'S LIFE

Something To Think About

Have you ever wondered what your pet—hamster, cat, dog, or fish—is thinking? Can people ever really understand how their pets think? Explain your answer.

Understanding the Poem Picture the boy in the poem, staring at his hamster in its cage.

- Why does the boy feel that his hamster's life is boring?
- What new idea makes the boy stop and think?

Just for Fun— Twisted Word Pairs

Any idea what "dreep" means? Try saying "drinks and sleeps" a few times. Then reverse the first two letters of each word. You've got it! "Slinks and dreeps"!

Have fun inventing other twisted word pairs. Here are some examples.

Note: Reverse the first one or two letters.

drives and snores	*becomes*	**snives and drores**
cries and laughs	*becomes*	**lies and craughs**
watches and thinks	*becomes*	_____
studies and plays	*becomes*	_____

Now create two of your own word pairs.

MORE GOOD READING

Coyotes in the Crosswalk: Canadian Wildlife in the City
by Diane Swanson

Coyotes in the crosswalk, frogs in the swimming pool, raccoons on the fire escape, garter snakes in the garage – Canada's cities are home to all these wild animals and many more. This fascinating book gives you all the facts. (a non-fiction book)

A Dog Called Dad
by Frank B. Edwards

"I was only a baby when the coyotes stole my Dad." So begins this hilarious picture book about a father raised by coyotes. When Dad came back, 8 years later, he chased cars and stole chickens for fun. What could his family do?! (a picture book)

Mister Got To Go
by Lois Simmie

One rainy night, a stray cat saw a cozy hotel and thought, "I'll just go inside and warm up." But the hotel manager warned, "Just until the rain stops. Then you've got to go!" Luckily, for Mister Got to Go, it rains a lot in Vancouver! (a picture book)

The Illustrated Father Goose
by Shelley Tanaka

This amazing book is based on a true story. Bill Lishman and his daughter teach a flock of Canada geese to fly with their ultra-light plane, then show the birds how to migrate south for the winter. You'll love the movie too—Fly Away Home! (a picture book)

EXPLORE!

Canoe Song

Traditional Song

My paddle's keen and bright,
flashing with silver.
Follow the wild goose flight.
Dip, dip and swing.

Dip, dip and swing her back,
flashing with silver.
Swift as the wild goose track.
Dip, dip and swing.

**BEFORE
YOU READ**

Flip through the pages of the story *A Dog Came, Too*. Take a quick look at the pictures, too. Now make a prediction: Is this a **true story** or a **fictional story**?

Hint: True stories are about people, places, and things that really exist (either now or in the past). Fictional stories are invented by the author.

Now read the story to find out if your prediction is right.

A Dog Came,

ONE

The Big Brown Dog

L ONG, LONG AGO, two native guides, an explorer, and seven voyageurs set off to find a route across Canada to the Pacific Ocean.

A big brown dog travelled with them.

He was not a pet. He was a working dog. All his life he had slept under the stars, not under a kitchen table.

He had never had his dinner served to him in a dog dish. He had never worn a collar or had a family to call his own.

The big brown dog didn't even have a name.

"Send Our Dog after him," the guides would say when they shot down a great white swan for food.

Too

"Our Dog will swim and fetch it," six voyageurs would say when the seventh voyageur dropped his paddle into a swift-flowing river.

"Our Dog will keep watch," the explorer would say when there were bears or wolves near the campsite.

The explorer, the voyageurs, and the guides grew more and more fond of Our Dog as they travelled toward the Pacific Ocean.

TWO

The Birchbark Canoe

IN THAT LONG, LONG-AGO TIME, the land was still covered with thick green forest. There were no roads to follow. The rivers were the roads, and the men followed them all the way across the vast land.

The explorer, the guides, and the voyageurs, plus all their food, boxes, and bundles took up a lot of room in the birchbark canoe. There was no space left for a big brown dog.

Our Dog didn't mind. He liked to run along the shore and sniff out little animals. He chased chipmunks, squirrels, rabbits, groundhogs, and gophers. Once he chased a porcupine. He didn't do it again.

The big brown dog loved the guides and he loved the voyageurs, but most of all he loved the explorer.

Our Dog would come quickly from far away whenever he heard the explorer's whistle.

Our Dog would perk up his ears and listen whenever he heard the explorer's voice.

Our Dog could tell when the explorer was worried. He could tell when he was lonely, too, or sad or happy.

Each night, under the stars, Our Dog would lie down by the explorer's side.

Our Dog was a guard dog at night, and so he slept very lightly. He was aware of every sound in the deep, dark forest.

Once he saw a wolf prowling a little too close to the sleeping men. He barked to warn them.

Once he discovered a hungry bear trying to take their food. He chased it away.

Another time he growled to warn the explorer when a stranger crept by the campsite on his hands and knees.

When the land was flat, Our Dog ran along the shore or on the open grasslands. He could always see the canoe, even from far away.

It was not as easy for the big brown dog when they reached the mountains. The canyons were deep and the rivers fast moving.

Sometimes Our Dog would swim along beside the speeding canoe, but the rapids were dangerous.

Sometimes he would run through the thick, dark forest high up the mountainside, and the canoe would shoot past him way down below.

THREE

The Friendly Village

IT WAS A LONG, LONG WAY to the Pacific Ocean. Our Dog grew very tired. His paws were cut by sharp, jagged rocks.

He was bitten by mosquitoes, wasps, blackflies, and fleas.

Sometimes there was little to eat, and there were no scraps for Our Dog. Tired and hungry, he would have to go hunting late at night for his meal.

The explorer, the voyageurs, and the native guides knew Our Dog was tired. They were tired, too. Often they had to carry their canoe and their boxes and bundles up one side of a mountain and down the other to avoid a dangerous rapid. They had little time or strength to sit by a warm fire removing burrs and twigs from Our Dog's tangled fur. They had little time or strength to look after their own comforts.

Then they came to a river that was worse than all the others. Our Dog could tell the explorer was worried. Time and time again they had to stop to repair the canoe. Eventually it was more patch than bark. It had become a patchwork canoe!

The men decided to leave that impossible river and travel overland to the ocean. New native guides they met in the mountains showed them a route that natives had travelled for hundreds of years.

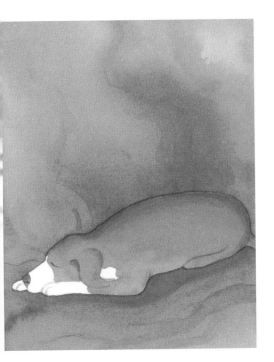

After many days they reached a cool, beautiful valley. Our Dog noticed a different smell in the air. It was the smell of salt water. The sea could not be far away.

Before the last lap of their journey the men rested and were treated kindly at a friendly native village. They ate well and they slept well.

Our Dog knew his friends were safe in the village. He did not lie down at the explorer's side. He limped wearily off into the forest and found a deep, dark cave. He curled up and fell sound asleep.

FOUR

The Deep, Dark Cave

OUR DOG SLEPT TOO WELL. The next morning the men were ready and eager to go on to the Pacific Ocean.

The explorer whistled. For the first time ever, Our Dog did not come. He did not hear the whistle in his deep, dark cave.

The voyageurs called and called. Still Our Dog did not come.

The guides searched the nearby forest, but they didn't find him. In his deep, dark cave Our Dog was sleeping more soundly than he had ever slept in his whole life.

The men were sad and worried, but they had to go on. Joined by more guides from the friendly village and equipped with more canoes, they set off down the river on the last lap of their journey. Our Dog slept on.

When he finally awoke the next day, he trotted down the hill to the friendly village. Our Dog's friends were nowhere to be found.

He tried to follow their scent, but he could not follow it past the water's edge. He laid his head down upon his matted paws and stared at the river. He felt lost and lonely. He whimpered and whined.

When darkness came, he howled mournfully. Eventually the villagers could stand the noise no longer. They chased him away.

Our Dog knew the explorer usually followed rivers. So he, too, followed the river to the Pacific Ocean.

Where the river met the ocean, high mountains rose up into the clouds on either side of a long inlet. Our Dog caught the scent of his friends. They had camped here. But they had moved on. Now they were far down the inlet, well out of sight ... and scent.

Again Our Dog laid his head down upon his matted paws. Again he whimpered and whined and howled. He was so sad and lonely that he stopped eating. He wandered up and down the river. He grew weaker and weaker.

The explorer, the voyageurs, and the guides had problems, too. Rain, fog, and high winds made travel dangerous.

One afternoon, when unfriendly-looking natives surrounded their canoes, the men were forced to land on a small rocky point. The explorer, the voyageurs, and the guides spent a sleepless night. Our Dog was not with them to warn of further danger.

In the morning the men were alarmed to see that more and more natives were landing on their rocky point. The voyageurs quickly packed up the canoes. But before they departed, the explorer painted a message on a rock. In years to come he hoped people would see his message and know he had truly reached the Pacific Ocean.

When Our Dog saw the explorer, the voyageurs, and the guides, who had returned up the river, he barked joyously.

Our Dog wagged his tail enthusiastically, but he was almost too weak and tired to stand up. The explorer knelt beside him, patted him gently, and whispered in his ear.

The voyageurs lifted Our Dog carefully and carried him to a canoe. Our Dog travelled as a passenger for the very first time.

With food and loving care, Our Dog recovered quickly. Soon he was well again and ready for the homeward journey all the way back across the vast country.

FIVE

The Journey Home

AFTER MANY WEEKS, as they neared the trading post that had been their starting point, Our Dog raced along the river's edge barking happily. The voyageurs began to paddle as fast as they could, while the explorer waved a big flag and the guides fired shots into the air.

They had travelled down rushing rivers and over snow-capped mountains. They had found the ocean they sought and they had returned safely. Now they prepared a huge feast to celebrate their journey. Our Dog sat by the fire with his nostrils twitching while his friends roasted a whole elk.

The guides allowed Our Dog to eat far more than his proper share of the tasty feast.

The voyageurs gave Our Dog seven hugs of thanks for all the help he had given them along the way.

And best of all, the explorer told him over and over again what a good dog he was.

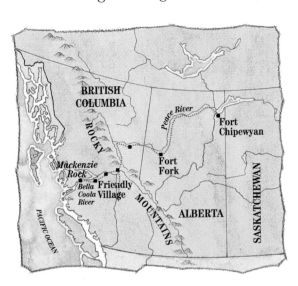

The explorer, whose name was Alexander Mackenzie, kept a diary on the long journey to the Pacific Ocean. He wrote about all his travels and trials. He also wrote about the big brown dog, and that is how we know his story.

With the help of many native people along the way, Alexander Mackenzie became the first European to cross North America by land. He reached the Pacific Ocean on the twenty-second day of July, 1793. Our Dog was the first dog to make the long journey west.

FOLLOW UP

Now's the time to decide: is *A Dog Came, Too* a true story, a fictional story, or both true and fictional at the same time? With your teacher, discuss the meaning of the phrase **historical fiction**.

How Did They Feel?

Congratulations!
You've finished reading
A Dog Came, Too.

Reading Between the Lines

Our Dog and the Explorer had many different feelings during their journey.

Sometimes they felt happy and excited, other times sad. Several times they felt frightened. Make a chart like this one in your notebook. Then fill in the times in the story when Our Dog and the Explorer felt happy, sad, or scared.

	Our Dog	The Explorer
Happy	When the journey began and he followed the canoe	
Sad		
Frightened		

Exploring with Our Dog

- Why do you think the explorer let Our Dog travel with him?

- What are some things Our Dog did to help out?

- How did the First Nations people help the explorer and the voyageurs?

- Did the explorer reach his goal on this voyage? What did he discover?

- What questions would you like to ask the explorer about his journey?

Did You Know ?

Early explorers in Canada discovered many useful things invented by First Nations people. Some examples are: birchbark canoes, toboggans, snowshoes, dogsleds, and kayaks. We still use these items today!

YOUR TURN TO WRITE

A Letter Home

When he was a young man, Alexander Mackenzie came to North America with his father, all the way from Scotland. Imagine that you are Alex Mackenzie. You have just returned from your journey to the Pacific coast, and you want to tell your sister all about it. You can't make a long-distance call, because telephones haven't been invented. But you can write her a letter. In your notebook or using a computer, write a letter telling your sister in Scotland all about Our Dog and your exciting trip through Western Canada. If you choose to use a computer, pick a font that makes your letter look like it was handwritten long ago.

TIP > **The Five Senses**
Describe what you saw, heard, tasted, smelled, and touched.

My dearest sister,

You fill in the letter

Your affectionate brother,
Alex

A Dog Came, Too

MEET AUTHOR
Ainslie Manson

. . . .

by Max Coles

Max: *I really enjoyed your story. Do you have a dog?*

Ainslie: Yes, two. I have a yellow Labrador called Calla and a black Labrador named Kenzie.

Max: *Is Kenzie named after the explorer, Alexander Mackenzie?*

Ainslie: Yes. That's because I got her in a special year—1993. Two hundred years earlier, in 1793, Alexander Mackenzie crossed Canada.

Max: *You seem to know a lot about Alexander Mackenzie.*

Ainslie: Now I do. It all began when I wrote a newspaper story about him. I began researching his life and his journeys. I read his journal, and that's where I first learned about his dog.

Max: *You mean the dog who followed his canoe?*

Ainslie: Yes, he's a real dog who travelled with Mackenzie on his journey. I knew as soon as I discovered him that I would have to write about him!

Max: *Did you follow part of Mackenzie's route?*

Ainslie: Yes, I wanted to walk in his footsteps. Part of the way I rode horseback. I also took lots of photographs. They were helpful to Ann Blades when she was doing the illustrations. Oh, and there was a dog on the trail with us! He belonged to one of the guides. I kept thinking, "This is just like Mackenzie's dog."

Max: *Did you see the place where he reached the Pacific?*

Ainslie: Yes, before writing the book, I went to the remote "rocky point" that I mentioned in my story. Seeing that spectacular spot really helped me to describe it.

Max: *How long did it take you to write the book?*

Ainslie: It only took me ten days. I'd been thinking about this story for a very long time. I think I had written it in my head before I sat down to write it.

Max: *Many of your stories take place in the past.*

Ainslie: I enjoy history, and I love sharing it with children. When I was in grade 10, I had a wonderful history teacher. She knew how to tell really interesting stories about things that happened long ago.

Max: *Did you write as a child?*

Ainslie: Yes, when I was about 10 years old, I began to keep a journal. It was like talking to a best friend. But I didn't often write stories.

Max: *Can you tell me a little about when and where you write?*

Ainslie: After breakfast I take my dogs on a good long walk. It clears my brain. Then I write from 9:00 till about noon. My room is bright and sunny with a view of the sea. But it's usually a terrible mess.

Max: *Do you have lots of story ideas?*

Ainslie: Yes, they all go in a wonderful wooden box called my Idea Box. I watch people all the time. I write down interesting things I see and hear, and I pop them all into the box. Photos, too. These ideas help inspire stories.

Max: *Do you have any advice for students who like to write?*

Ainslie: Start your own Idea Box. And write every day. Keep a private journal and write just what you think. If you keep it up, you'll find your own special voice. ◆

Look for Ainslie Manson's picture book, *Just Like New*. It takes place in Montréal during World War II.

BEFORE YOU READ

Before you read this article, collect a street map of your town, a map of Canada, an atlas, and a globe of the world. Do you know how to use these items?

MAPS AND MAPPING

Text adapted from Barbara Taylor

FINDING A PLACE ON A MAP

Have you ever tried to find a street on a map, or a town in an atlas? The easiest way is to use the index. The number and letter combinations (**1A**, **4D**) give the **grid square**.

Atlas of Canada - Index		
Tobermory, Ont.	page 41	**1A**
Tofield, Alta.	page 111	**4D**
Tofino, B.C.	page 112	**4F**
Tompkins, Sask.	page 110	**3E**
Torbay, Nfld.	page 103	**5D**
Torngat Mountains, Que.	page 49	**10C**

Here's how grid squares work. On the map below, you can see vertical lines and horizontal lines. When the lines cross, they create squares. To find 5C, run your finger along from the number 5. Run another finger down from the letter C. Where your fingers meet is the square 5C.

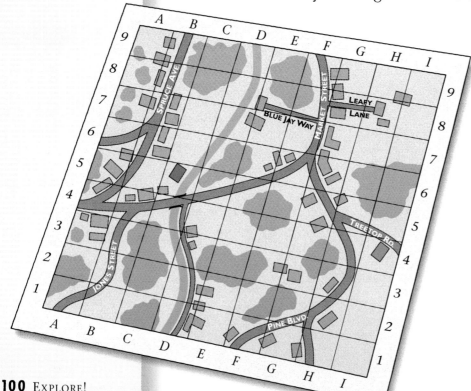

Try it yourself!

1. In what grid square do Market Street and Jones Street meet?

2. In what grid square do Pine Boulevard and Treetop Road meet?

   (The answers are upside down at the bottom of the page.)

Answers: 1. 4B and 2. 5H

DO IT YOURSELF

Let's say you want to meet your friends in an exact spot in the park. See if you can make a map with grid squares to mark the meeting spot.

1. Draw a rough map of your local park on large-squared graph paper. Or draw the grid lines yourself.

2. Label the grid squares across the top and bottom and up the sides. Use letters and numbers, as on the map below.

3. Work out a meeting place, and tell your friends the grid square.

You could also create a map to tell your friends where you buried some treasure!

Archaeologists make a grid on the ground using strings. Then they make a map with a matching grid. When they find something interesting, they can mark the exact spot on the map. This helps them to remember exactly where each object was discovered.

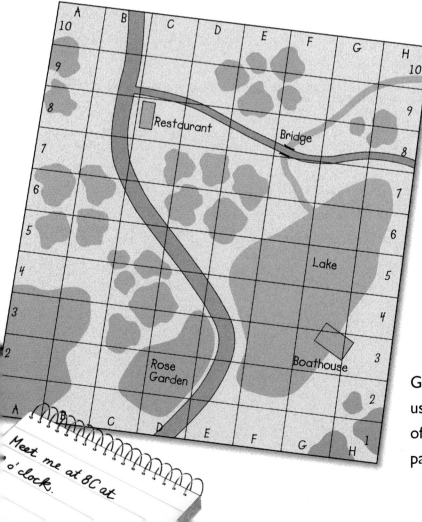

Globes and maps of the world also use grid lines. They are called lines of latitude and longitude. Turn the page to find out more about them.

LATITUDE AND LONGITUDE

On globes and maps of the world, we can find a place by using a grid of imaginary lines. These lines are called lines of latitude and longitude.

Lines of Latitude—Parallels

These lines run east-west around the Earth. They are like circles drawn around a ball. Latitude is measured in degrees (°) north or south of the equator, a line that circles the Earth's middle. The equator is 0° latitude.

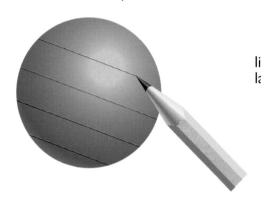

North Pole

60°N

30°N

South

0°
Equator

North

lines of latitude

30°S

60°S

South Pole

Lines of Longitude—Meridians

These lines run north-south between the North Pole and the South Pole. They are like half circles drawn around a ball. Longitude is measured in degrees (°) east or west of a line drawn through Greenwich, in England. This line, called prime meridian, is 0° longitude.

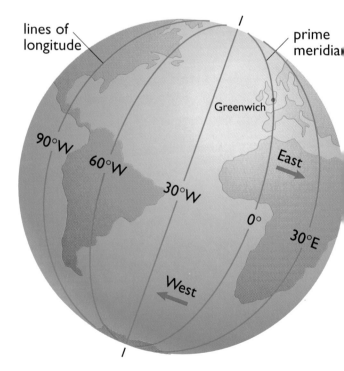

lines of longitude

prime meridian

Greenwich

90°W

60°W

East

30°W

0°

30°E

West

FINDING A PLACE USING LATITUDE AND LONGITUDE

Lines of latitude and longitude form a grid around the Earth. This grid makes it possible to find any place on the Earth's surface.

The latitude of a place tells where that place is located, north or south of the equator. For example, 45°N.

The longitude tells where a place is located, east or west of the prime meridian. For example, 75°W.

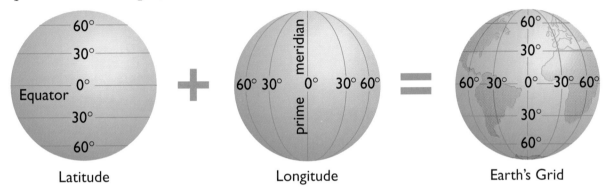

Latitude + Longitude = Earth's Grid

Find the Town

Look at the globe on the right.

A Canadian town is located at **45°N, 75°W**.

Can you find out its name using a real globe in your classroom?

(The answer is upside down at the bottom of this page)

What is the latitude and longitude of your town?

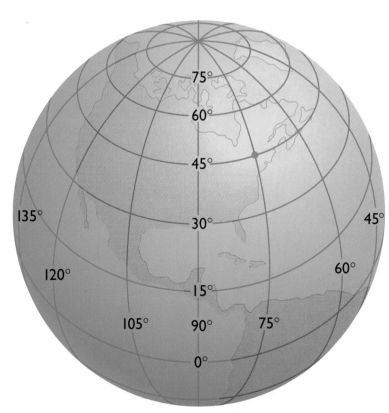

The answer is Cornwall, Ontario.

Maps and Mapping **103**

FINDING THE WAY

Maps tell us which direction to take (north, south, east or west) to reach a place. In other words, maps help us to find our way.

On most maps, north is at the top. But if you are walking across country with a map, and you want to know which way to go, you need a compass as well.

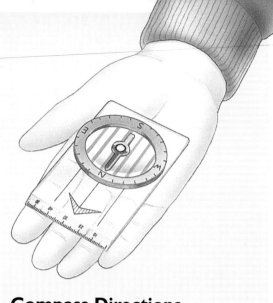

Compass Directions

The four main points on a compass are North, South, East, and West. The needle of the compass is a tiny magnet that always points North.

USING A MAP AND COMPASS

Suppose you want to walk south to a bridge.

I. Place a compass on your map.

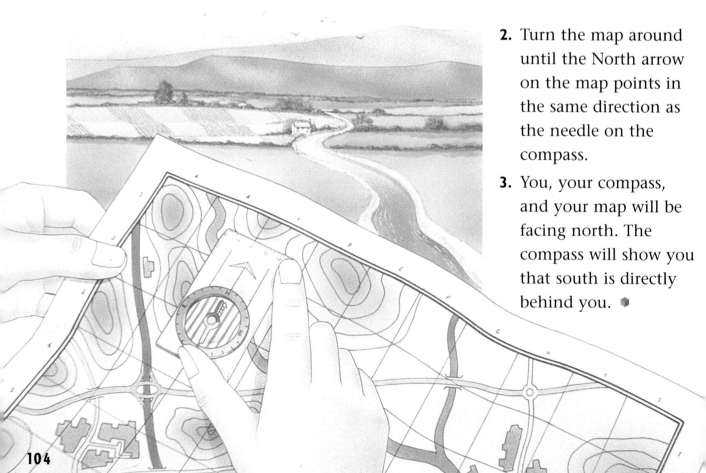

2. Turn the map around until the North arrow on the map points in the same direction as the needle on the compass.

3. You, your compass, and your map will be facing north. The compass will show you that south is directly behind you. 🔹

Think about what you have learned about street maps, country maps, atlases, and globes of the world. Which ones do you think you will use most often? Why?

Applying Information

Locating Yourself

1. On a street map of your town: Locate the street where you live, using the index and the grid squares. In what grid square is your home?

2. On a map of Canada or in an atlas: Locate your town. What are the nearest lines of latitude and longitude?

3. On a map of North America or a globe: Locate Canada. What line of latitude follows most of the border between Canada and the United States? (*Answer below*)

Go for a Country Hike

Ask some grown-ups to help you arrange a class hike in the country. You will need strong shoes or boots, a backpack for your lunch, and several adult companions. Take a map and a compass with you. Practise using them to follow the trail. They should help you not to get lost!

Did You Know

An arrow on a map points to "true north," the North Pole. But a compass needle points to "magnetic north." Magnetic north is about 1600 km away from the true North Pole! Serious hikers must take this difference into account.

The answer is 49°N—also called the 49th parallel.

VIKINGS, HO!

STORY BY SUSAN HUGHES
PICTURES BY DAVID DAY

MEGAN AND HER FAMILY ARE VISITING THE VIKING SITE AT L'ANSE AUX MEADOWS, IN NEWFOUNDLAND...

The Vikings were the first Europeans to reach North America. They landed here in Newfoundland.

Columbus landed in A.D. 1492. But the Vikings arrived almost 500 years before that!

I thought Christopher Columbus came first.

Megan, don't you know anything!

 The Vikings were great shipbuilders. Many of them sailed from Norway to look for better farmland and timber. One group settled in Iceland. Others, like Eric the Red, went to Greenland. It is likely that the Vikings were the first Europeans ever to set foot on these icy lands, too! The first to cross the Atlantic Ocean was Bjarni Herjolfson, but he didn't land.

Greenland

Iceland

Norway

Atlantic Ocean

Newfoundland

Ouch! What's this?

109

Understanding the Story

"Time Travel" Storyboard

The beginning and ending of this story take place in modern times. The events in between took place about 1000 years ago, when Megan travelled back through time. To show how well you have understood the story, make a storyboard.

1. Fold a large piece of paper into eight sections and number them.

2. In box 1, tell the beginning of the story and draw a picture of it (an example has been done for you).

3. In box 8, write the ending and illustrate it.

4. Next, decide on the six most important story events in between. Tell them in order in boxes 2 to 7. Illustrate all of these events, too.

5. In a group of four, share your storyboards.

Media Link

Design a Movie Poster

Imagine that you have made a movie of the cartoon story, *Vikings, Ho!* You want to encourage lots of people to come and see your movie. Design a poster that creates a sense of action and excitement. You may wish to use a computer draw or paint application to design your poster.

You will need
- a title in big, bold letters
- an illustration of a scene from the movie
- the names of the actors you've chosen to star in the movie
- a line such as: "Coming Soon to a Theatre Near You!"

Make a Diagram

Viking Ships

Viking ships were both seaworthy and beautiful. Draw your own diagram of Leif the Lucky's ship, using details from the story and books from the library for help. When you have finished your diagram, label the parts of the ship.

Find Out More About...

Find out more about the Vikings in your library or on the Internet. Choose one of the topics below. Then create a one- or two-page cartoon story to tell what you've learned.

The Vikings Go Exploring

Viking Home Life

A Visit to L'Anse aux Meadows, Newfoundland

TIP ⟩ **Cartoons**

Think before you begin: How much of a cartoon story is told through the pictures, and how much through the words?

Trip → to
the Seashore

Poem by
Lois Simmie

Picture by
Dušan Petricić

We drove to the seashore,
My ma and pa,
Brother Bertie
And Sue and me;
From Biggar,
Saskatchewan,
Over the mountains,
What did we see?
We saw the sea.

Sister Sue said
"Isn't it big?
It's bigger than Biggar
Or anything yet."
Brother Bertie
Up to his knees,
And Ma to her ankles
Said "Isn't it wet?"

I let out a yelp
When I saw kelp
And a scuttling crab,
Pa laughed at that;
He sat on the land
With his toes in the sand,
"I'll be darned," he said,
"Isn't it flat?"

116

RESPONDING

to TRIP TO THE SEASHORE

Geography Connection

Personal Connection Ma, Pa, Bertie, Sue, and the poet went exploring by car. What new things did they discover? What part of the trip was the most fun?

In a small group, tell about a trip you have taken. Where did you go and what did you see? Share your stories with the class.

The family in the poem saw three kinds of geographical regions on their trip:

1. the Prairies

2. the Rocky Mountains

3. the Pacific Ocean

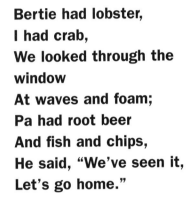

At the seafood restaurant
Ma had oysters,
They looked horrid,
Green and squishy;
There were boats through the
window,
Sue had scallops,
(Pa said we had to have
Something fishy).

Bertie had lobster,
I had crab,
We looked through the
window
At waves and foam;
Pa had root beer
And fish and chips,
He said, "We've seen it,
Let's go home."

We drove all day
We travelled all night,
The parents and Sue
And Bertie and I;
We fought over comics
And seashells and Pa yelled
"Look at the mountains!
Aren't they high?"

We got home to Biggar,
Ma and Pa,
Sister Sue
And Bertie and me;
Pa said "Look,
Isn't it beautiful?
Big and flat,
Just like the sea."

- In what Canadian provinces can you find each of these regions?

- The Prairies and the ocean are very different, but Pa noticed that in one way they are the same. In what way are they the same?

- On a map, find the family's starting point—Biggar, Saskatchewan. Then work out the route they might have driven to get to the sea.

Trip to the Seashore **117**

Going Underground is an article from a magazine. Scan the article before you read. Here's how:

- Take a look at the **photographs**.

- Find the **title** and the three **sub-headings**.

- Find the two **sidebars** with special information: "A spelunker's delight" and "Stalactites and Stalagmites."

Now you have a good idea of what the article is about: exploring caves!

Going Underground

Article by Diane Bailey and Drew McKibben

THE THIN BEAM from my headlamp projects a circle of light onto the grey rock that surrounds me. I'm on my stomach, slithering through a narrow tunnel deep inside the Selkirk Mountains of British Columbia, in a place called Cody Caves (*above*). My helmet scrapes on the low-hanging ceiling. I put my head down and inch forward.

At the end of the four-metre-long tunnel, I crawl out into a small room with sharp, jagged rock walls. Ten-year-old Jordan and his dad, Drew, are already there, wondering where to go next. It looks like a dead end. Then our guide points to a tiny, dark opening in the floor. We're going through there? Wait a minute, we're going through there?!

Jordan (*below*) eagerly lowers himself into the hole and disappears from sight. Sometimes it pays to be a kid. The adults have a tougher time. We twist and turn, trying to keep from getting stuck. Once through, we flip over onto our backs and scramble down a steep passageway feet first, noses almost touching the ceiling. Luckily, it only takes a few seconds to get to the large cavern below.

Going Underground **119**

Beneath the Earth

Going underground is like discovering a whole new world. The first thing we notice is the chill. The temperature inside a cave is the same as the surrounding rock, which in Cody Caves is 7°C. That's as cold as the inside of your refrigerator. The air feels damp. Water drips from the ceiling and walls. I flash my light on the wall beside me and the droplets sparkle like gold.

Deep inside the cave, it's pitch dark. We decide to see just how dark it is, and turn out our headlamps. Jordan is sitting right beside me. I hear him breathing, but I can't see him. I put my hand up a few centimetres from my face. I see only blackness.

Buried in this deep gloom is a landscape of incredible beauty. With our lights back on we scan the delicate rock formations that cling to the ceilings and stretch up from the floors, some as much as half a metre tall. Waterfalls tumble over low stone walls. Seemingly endless caverns, corridors, and twisting tunnels connect to form a complicated maze. An underground creek noisily weaves its way along the floor.

This is a world that has taken millions of years to create.

Cave Decorations

The Central Chamber is the largest room in Cody Caves. It's about the size of a small house. When we get there, we look up in amazement. Dozens of thin, white stone tubes (*right*) are hanging from the grey rock eight metres above. These tubes are called soda straws and are one of the many unusual and beautiful decorations that sprout from the ceilings, walls, and floors of all limestone caves.

In Cody Caves, it takes 100 years for decorations to grow one cubic centimetre—that's smaller than a sugar cube! In one of the smaller rooms, we come across a short, fat stalagmite that's no bigger than a wastebasket (*far left*). Our guide figures it's been growing for millions of years.

Stalactites and Stalagmites

Limestone caves like Cody Cave have all kinds of amazing decorations. These shapes start with dripping water that contains dissolved limestone (calcite). Then they keep growing slowly, year after year. The most famous formations are stalactites and stalagmites.

stalactites: large stone "icicles" that hang from the ceiling

stalagmites: cone-shaped columns that form on the floor

Sometimes stalactites and stalagmites meet in the middle to form thick columns.

A Spelunker's Delight

(a spelunker explores caves as a hobby)

Caving is exciting, but it can also be dangerous. It's easy to get lost underground going from cavern to cavern, or to slip and hurt yourself on wet, jagged rocks. You should never enter a cave alone or unprepared. The best way to explore a cave is to go with an experienced guide. If caving interests you, here is a list of caves you might want to visit.

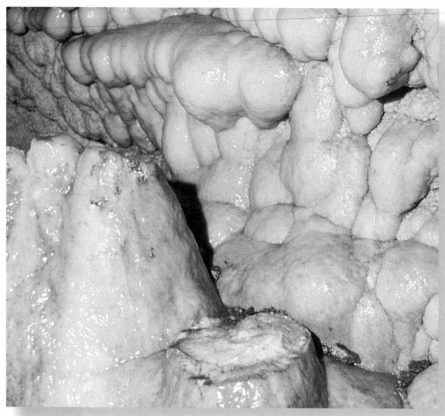

Cody Caves Provincial Park is located in the Selkirk Mountains, about 40 km north of Nelson, British Columbia.

Horne Lake Caves Provincial Park is located near Qualicum Beach on Vancouver Island.

Bonnechere Caves are located 8 km south of Eganville, Ontario. The galleries and passages are all lighted.

La Grotte de Saint-Elzéar in Québec features some beautiful formations.

La Caverne de Saint-Léonard is a small cave close to downtown Montréal.

Laflèche Caves are located about 30 minutes north of Hull, Québec. They are the largest caves in the Canadian Shield.

It seems that everybody knows about stalagmites and stalactites. But what about cave pearls and bacon strips? Have you ever heard of moon milk (*above*) or boxwork? Cavers use these names to describe some of the remarkable formations we saw in Cody Caves. They all have different shapes, even though they're all formed when water leaves behind the bits of calcite it's carrying.

The Caver's Motto

Caves are treasures of time. But people haven't always treated them like treasures. Thoughtless visitors paint on cave walls, carve their names on rocks, and leave trash behind. In Cody Caves, we saw stumps of stalactites that were broken off by souvenir hunters.

Serious cavers also have to be careful. One wrong step can destroy a stalagmite. One careless arm movement can snap a stalactite. Even a touch can do damage: the oil on our skin will stop the growth of cave decorations. "This is probably the most fragile environment you'll ever be in," says our guide.

After two hours underground, we climb out of the cave and take a deep breath of fresh air. The sun feels warm on our faces. It takes a moment for our eyes to adjust to its bright light. It's nice to be back on familiar ground, but none of us would have missed this chance to uncover the secrets of the hidden depths.

If you go underground, remember the caver's motto: cave softly. By exploring carefully, you can help preserve this remarkable subterranean world for future visitors. ◆

As you read the article, did you

- use the **photos** to help you understand the text?

- see that the **sub-heads** signalled a change of topic?

- notice that the **sidebars** contained extra information?

Good! You're learning to use **text features** to help you read.

Understanding the Article

Getting in Deeper

- How did they get down to the main cavern? What was the scariest thing they had to do?

- Reread "Beneath the Earth." How cold is it inside the cave? How dark is it? What did the group see when they turned on their headlamps?

- Explain the difference between stalactites and stalagmites.

- List four other kinds of cave decorations described in "Cave Decorations."

- What is "The Caver's Motto"? Why is it necessary?

- Which of the caves in "A Spelunker's Delight" is nearest to your home?

- Why do some people enjoy caving? Give three reasons for your answer.

Congratulations! You're now a member of the Underground Readers' Club!

READ LIKE A WRITER

Action Verbs

The authors really wanted you to feel what it was like going down into Cody Cave. To do this they used great action verbs like "slithering." Find six more action verbs that give the feeling of pushing through some very tight places.

TIP > Don't forget to use exciting action verbs when you write your own story about exploring!

A computer database is a great way to start a word bank of action words for you and your classmates to use.

A Story About Exploring

Think about a time when you went exploring. Perhaps you explored your own neighbourhood with friends, or took a car trip to somewhere new with the family, or explored a beach or a forest on your summer holidays.

- When you're ready to write, brainstorm some exciting action verbs.

- Make your story short and snappy.

- Use action verbs to make your readers feel the excitement you felt.

Give a Talk

You have learned enough about caves and cavers to give a short "off the cuff" speech (no need for notes or preparation). Work with a partner and take turns. One of you will speak for one minute while the other listens.

Decorations in Cody Caves

Why Caving is Exciting

The Dangers of Careless Caving

This Canada

Poem by
Maxine Tynes

Picture by
Susan Todd

Tell me what this country is
this Canada
this nation of same and different
 of faces and voices and places
  and trees
 of east and west
 of Inuit, Aboriginal
 of French and English
 and everyone else in between.

Tell me what this country feels
this Canada
this nation of together and separate
 of push and pull
 of *bonjour* and good morning
 of stars and stripes beckoning
 of northern lights showing tears
 of the first people.

Show me a map of this country
this Canada
charted with a past that beckons
 and keeps us
charted with rivers of hopes
 and dreams
shaped by winds of change
shaded with the faces of you and of us
as we move toward new freedoms
as we come into our own
This Canada.

Home Link

Explore Your Heritage

The first people living in Canada were the Inuit and First Nations people. Then came the French-speaking people from France, and later, the English-speaking people from Britain. Finally, people from all over the world came to live here. Where do you and your family come from? How long has your family been in Canada? As a class, make a chart showing all the countries you came from.

An Idea to Explore

Maxine Tynes writes that the map of Canada is "charted with rivers of hopes and dreams." What hopes and dreams do you have for Canada?

Make an Illustrated Map

Work in a small group. Make a big outline map of Canada. Then fill it with cut-out pictures of Canadian faces, young and old.

MORE GOOD READING

A Canoe Trip
by Bobbie Kalman

You can take a canoe trip by reading this book. It's full of exciting photographs of kids like you. Read along as they learn to paddle, carry the canoe (portage), pitch tents, cook meals, and "bear-proof" their camp! Hike and swim, too. (a non-fiction book)

Forts of Canada
by Ann-Maureen Owens and Jane Yealland

This book will take you inside all kinds of early Canadian forts. Visit a voyageur fort, where Mackenzie might have stayed. Find out how the forts were built, how people worked and played in forts, and how to make model forts. (a non-fiction book)

Last Leaf First Snowflake to Fall
by Leo Yerxa

A parent and child take us on a dreamlike canoe trip into nature. Beautiful collage pictures reveal rivers and islands and colourful forests at autumn's close. At the end, all is silenced by snow. (a poetic picture book)

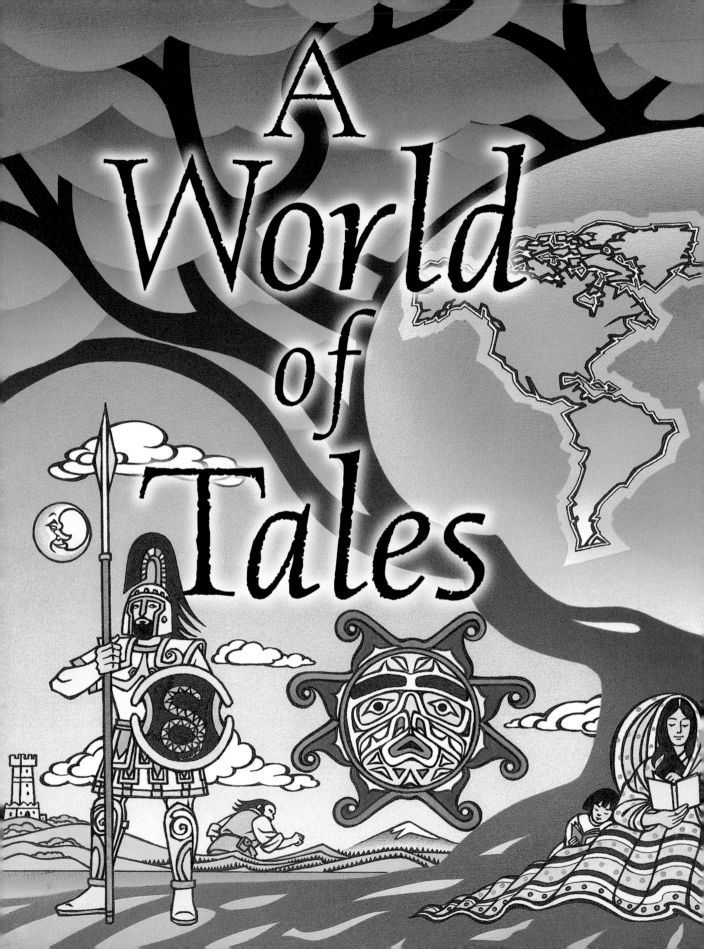

Children Just Like Me: Our Favourite Stories
by Jamila Given

Crow and Fox and Other Animal Legends
by Jan Thornhill

How we saw the world: Nine Native stories of the way things began
by C. J. Taylor

Realms of Gold: Myths and Legends from Around the World
by Ann Pilling

129

How Eagle Man created the islands of the Pacific Coast

A BELLA COOLA LEGEND

by C. J. Taylor

ONCE LONG AGO all the people in a village became very selfish. They did not help their neighbours. They did not share food. They did not even take very good care of their children.

One day the father and mother of a boy left to go hunting and never returned. The boy did not know whether they had been killed or had just gone off and forgotten him. Desperate and alone, he went to his nearest relative, an uncle, for help.

The uncle didn't want to have anything to do with the orphaned boy. "I have no time to care for this boy," he announced. "Does anyone want to adopt him? If not, let the whole village look after him. I'm not going to do it."

The villagers refused to help. "If you won't look after him, why should we? Don't bother us with your problems." The uncle, who was not only selfish but cruel as well, decided to get rid of his nephew. He took the boy down to the beach and put him in a canoe. "Sleep here tonight," he ordered. "You'll be comfortable. It's cooler than inside."

When the boy fell asleep, the uncle cut the canoe adrift and watched it float off toward the ocean. "That's the last I'll see of him," he thought, pleased with himself.

THE WATER CARRIED THE CANOE far along the shore and finally up onto a beach near the village of the Eagle people. They were kind and they welcomed the boy as if he were sent as a gift. Everyone cared for him and he grew up to be a fine young man. The chief's daughter fell in love with him, and when they were married the chief gave him the name of Eagle Man, a cloak of feathers and a very special present: he was taught how to fly.

Eagle Man was happy with his new family, but he could not completely forget the people in the village who had refused to care for him and the uncle who had tried to get rid of him. As he grew older, the memory came back to haunt him day and night. "I must go back there," he told his wife. "I must."

Eagle Man put on his feather cloak and flew to the village where he was born. As he passed over it, he caught sight of his uncle and was overcome with anger. He swooped down, caught the cruel man by the hair and lifted him off the ground.

A villager saw this and tried to hold the uncle back by grabbing at his feet. He too was lifted up. Soon the entire village was hanging onto each other and being carried off.

Eagle Man flew over the ocean and began dropping the villagers one by one into the water. "You did not love and care for each other when you were together," he told them. "Now you will be separated from each other forever."

As the villagers fell into the water, each became an island. That is why on the Northwest Coast, there are thousands of islands, all separated by water. ◗

How Eagle Man created the islands of the Pacific Coast

C. J. Taylor

by Paul Currdina

C. J. Taylor was excited when she discovered her family history.

Named Carrie Jo at birth, C. J. grew up in a small town near Montréal. Her mother came from a German-British family, but her father was Mohawk, from the Akwesasne reserve. He grew up knowing very little about his heritage.

When she was five years old, C. J. met her father's mother for the first time. "I was fascinated with my grandmother," says C. J. "She looked just like Geronimo. He was a famous Apache leader whose picture I'd seen in my mother's history books. Suddenly I realized that my grandmother's history was my history, too."

Even as a small child, C. J. loved to draw and paint. After her own children went to school, she found time to start painting again. She remembered the photographs she had seen as a girl. "It seemed natural for me to paint the faces and headdresses of my ancestors," says C. J.

Now C. J. is an author as well as an artist. She has written and illustrated many books for children. She travels across Canada and the United States talking to kids about the stories and art of First Nations people.

As a little girl, C. J. wondered who her people were. Now she is telling the stories her father never knew. "Looking back over my life, I realize how lucky I am. I was blessed with the talent to tell the stories of my people."

Look in the library for some of C. J. Taylor's story collections, including *How Two-Feather was saved from loneliness*, *The ghost and lone warrior*, *Little Water and the gift of the animals*, *How we saw the world*, and her latest book, *Messenger of spring*.

BEFORE YOU READ

Find Japan on a globe or a map of the world. What province of Canada is closest to Japan? Read on to discover what wonder of nature this Japanese legend explains.

A Japanese Legend Retold by Florence Sakade
Pictures by Tomio Nitto

The Spider Weaver

LONG AGO there was a young farmer named Yosaku. One day he was working in the fields and saw a snake getting ready to eat a spider. Yosaku felt very sorry for the spider, so he ran at the snake with his hoe and drove the snake away, saving the spider's life. Then the spider disappeared into the grass, but first it stopped for a moment to bow in thanks to Yosaku.

ONE MORNING not long after that, Yosaku was in his house when he heard a tiny voice outside calling, "Mr. Yosaku! Mr. Yosaku!" He went to the door and saw a young girl standing in the yard.

"I heard you are looking for someone to weave cloth for you," said the girl. "Won't you please let me work here and weave for you?"

Yosaku was very pleased because he really did need a weaver. So he showed the girl the weaving room and she started to work at the loom. At the end of the day Yosaku went to see what she'd done and was very surprised to find that she'd woven eight long pieces of cloth, enough to make eight kimonos! He'd never known anyone could weave so much in just a single day.

"How ever did you weave so much?" he asked the girl.

But instead of answering him, she said a very strange thing: "You mustn't ask me that. And you must never come into the weaving room while I am at work."

But Yosaku was very curious. So one day he slipped very quietly up to the weaving room and peeped in the window. What he saw really surprised him. Because it was not the girl seated at the loom, but a large spider, weaving very fast with its eight legs, and for thread it was using its own spider web, which came out of its mouth.

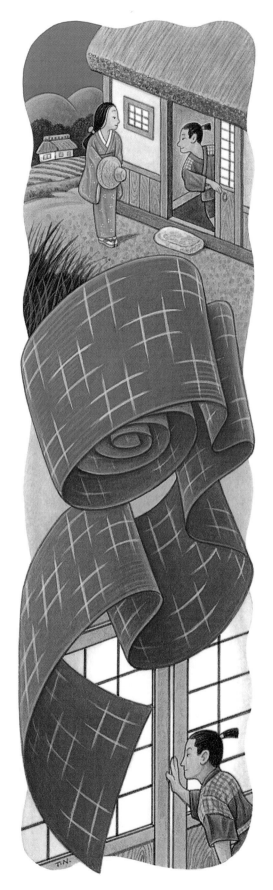

The Spider Weaver 135

YOSAKU LOOKED VERY CLOSELY and saw that it was the same spider which he'd saved from the snake. Then Yosaku understood. The spider had been so thankful that it had wanted to do something to help Yosaku. So it had turned itself into a human and asked to weave cloth for him. Just by eating the cotton in the weaving room it could spin it into thread inside its own body, and then with its eight legs it could weave the thread into cloth very, very fast.

Yosaku was very grateful for the spider's help. He noticed that the cotton was almost used up. So the next morning he set out for the nearest village, on the other side of the mountains, to buy some more cotton. He bought a big bundle of cotton and started home, carrying it on his back.

Along the way a very terrible thing happened. Yosaku sat down to rest, and the very same snake that he'd driven away from the spider came up and slipped inside the bundle of cotton. But Yosaku didn't know anything about this. So he carried the cotton home and gave it to the weaving girl.

The weaving girl was very glad to get the cotton, because she'd used up all the cotton that was left. So she took the bundle and went to the weaving room.

As soon as the girl was inside the room she turned back into a spider and began eating the cotton very fast, just as though it were something delicious to eat, so she could spin it into thread. The spider ate and ate and ate. Suddenly, when it got down to the bottom of the bundle, the snake jumped out of the cotton. It opened its mouth wide to swallow the spider. The spider was very frightened and jumped out of the window. The snake went wriggling very fast after it. And the spider had eaten so much cotton that it couldn't run very fast. So the snake gradually caught up with the spider. Again the snake opened its mouth wide to gulp the spider down. But just then a wonderful thing happened.

The Sun, up in the sky, had been watching what was happening. He knew how kind the spider had been to Yosaku and he felt very sorry for the poor little spider. So he reached down with a sunbeam and caught hold of the end of the spider's web and lifted the spider high up into the sky, where the snake couldn't reach it at all.

The spider was very grateful to the Sun for saving it from the snake. So it used all the cotton that was inside its body to weave beautiful fluffy clouds up in the sky.

That's the reason, they say, why clouds are soft and white like cotton; and that is also the reason why a spider and a cloud are called by the same name in Japan—kumo. ⬡

Good Reading! You've just read two legends. Now let's compare them!

Something to Think About

"How" and "Why" Legends

Long ago, people created legends to explain the world of nature. These legends told "how" and "why" natural things came to be —like thunderstorms and seasons.

Nowadays, we have different explanations of nature. Science explains how islands emerge from the sea, how clouds form fluffy white shapes, and how rainbows get their colours. But we still love to hear and read the old legends. Maybe it's because they contain true lessons about people and how we should treat each other.

Why do you think we still enjoy legends?

Understanding the Story

A Legend Told Around the Fire

Imagine the Bella Coola people long ago, sitting around their cooking fire. An old woman looks out over the ocean and begins to speak:

"Do you know where all those islands came from," she asks.

"Yes," the children cry. "But tell us again!" And so she tells them the legend of *How Eagle Man created the islands of the Pacific Coast*. Her story explains how the islands came to be. But it also teaches other lessons about families and communities.

- According to the legend, how did the Pacific Coast islands come to be?

- Team up with a partner. Talk about the other lessons that this legend teaches.

A Legend Told at Harvest Time

Long ago, a Japanese family gathers for their evening meal. After everyone has finished eating, the children beg for a story. So Grandfather tells the tale of *The Spider Weaver*. He explains that he first heard the story from his grandfather, and so on, back in time forever.

- According to the legend, why are clouds soft and white? Why are spiders and clouds called by the same name in Japan?

- What other lessons did you learn from this legend?

A "How" or "Why" Legend

Imagine that you are living long, long ago. You want to understand how or why something came to be the way it is. Here are some examples:

- How the Beaver Got Its Tail
- Why Earthquakes Happen
- Why the River Floods

With a partner, brainstorm lots of other examples. Then choose one "how" or "why" idea and create a legend that explains it.

1. Talk about your ideas for the legend with your partner.

2. Write a first draft of your legend.

3. Read it to your partner. Listen to his or her suggestions. Then switch places.

4. Revise your legend so that it tells your story well.

5. With your partner, correct your spelling and punctuation.

TIP Story Starters:
- Your title could begin with "How" or "Why."
- Your story could begin with "Long ago, ..."

Find Kenya on a
map of Africa.
What animals
would you see if
you could visit
Kenya?

To enjoy this comic
folk tale, ask your
teacher to read it
aloud for you.
Then sit back and
chuckle!

A FOLK TALE
FROM KENYA
BY HEATHER
FOREST

PICTURES BY
CLARENCE
PORTER

The Man Who Could Transform Himself

There were once two brothers who were very poor.
They were orphans and had nothing in the world to
sustain them but two cows. One day the older brother took
both cows to a magician and said, "I will trade you these
two cows if you can give me some magical powers."

"One must know how to use the powers wisely," said
the magician, eyeing the cattle.

"I will be careful and use the powers to help others,"
said the older brother.

"Very well then, I will teach you how to transform yourself into any animal you want to be," said the magician, taking the two cows as payment.

When the brother had received a charm to change himself, he ran home as fast as his legs would carry him. He became tired as he ran and, transforming himself into a bird, he soared home. He landed on the ground in front of his younger brother and changed himself back into a man.

The younger brother gasped in amazement at what his brother could now do, but then he noticed that his brother had returned without the cows. He cried, "What use is this magic to us? We have no way to eat! At least before we could milk the cows!"

"Fear not, young brother," said the older one confidently. "You will soon see how I will use my powers to our benefit. Tomorrow when you look out of the window of our house you will see a great bull. It will be Me! Take me to market and sell me for two cows and five goats. Do not disobey me! Do not tell anyone about my powers."

"I will do as you say," said the younger brother, curious to see the plan his brother had in mind.

The next morning, when the younger brother looked out of his window, there was a huge bull standing in the field. He walked to the bull and tied a rope around his neck. As he led the beast off to the marketplace, everyone exclaimed at his size. A rich man bought the bull for two cows and five goats. He planned to give the bull as a wedding gift to his bride's family. Delighted with the sale, the younger brother drove the cows and goats he had been paid to his own home.

The rich man tried to lead the bull down the road, but the animal charged him, knocked him down, and ran away. The bull galloped and bellowed. He snorted and ran. Clouds of dust rose at his hooves. The man chased after the bull and bellowed just as loudly, "Come back! Come back!"

When the bull was out of sight, he turned the front half of himself into a lion. The footprints on the road were a confusion of bull and lion. Then he turned himself back into a man and sat calmly down beside the road. The rich man came huffing and puffing. "Have you seen a bull run by?" he asked the older brother.

"Yes," said the older brother, "a lion chased him. Look at the tracks!"

"Woe is me!" cried the rich man. "See how the lion had already eaten my bull. There was a great struggle! Now I've lost my bride's gift!"

The rich man turned sadly for home as the older brother jogged off, delighted with his greedy trick.

The next day the older brother wanted more goats and cows and said to his younger brother, "Let us do our market trading again. I will become a bull again. This time, trade me for three cows and eight goats. Soon we will be rich!"

In a blink, a huge bull was before the younger brother, who by now stood in awe of his older brother's power. He led the bull to market and immediately received the price he asked from a tall man who was delighted with the fine animal. "Come now," he said to the bull, "soon you will be a great feast."

The tall man drove the bull down the road to where he planned to slaughter him. But the bull began to run as before. He galloped and bellowed. He snorted and ran 'til the dust was a cloud at his hooves. The tall man ran after him shouting, "Come back! Come back!"

The bull stopped and faced the tall man. With a great snort, he turned himself into a lion and began to roar, thinking that this would frighten the tall man away.

But unknown to the older brother, the tall man who had purchased him was the magician in disguise. The tall man immediately turned himself into a lion too. He roared and charged.

The bull who had become a lion quickly turned himself into a bird. He flew upwards until his wings brushed the sky. The magician turned himself into a hawk and pursued the bird. He swooped and soared. His sharp claws almost clutched the small bird. The bird quickly swerved down to the ground and turned himself into an antelope. He leaped and sprang and dashed away. The hawk swooped down and turned himself into a wolf. He loped after the antelope, his jaws drooling for a fine meal. The antelope could feel the wolf's hot breath on his neck and knew that he was lost. In desperation he turned back into a man and pleaded, "Please do not kill me. You can have all your cows and goats back!"

The wolf turned into the magician and said, "Give me back the charm and all of your goats and cows. Then I will spare your life."

The older brother gave the magician the charm, the cows, and the goats. He lost his power and he lost his herd. A trickster must be careful whom he tricks. ◆

THE Hummingbirds' Gift

A Folk Tale from Mexico
by Stefan Czernecki
and Timothy Rhodes

BEFORE YOU READ

In Mexico, there is a village called Tzintzuntzan, which is famous for its hummingbirds. Thousands of hummingbirds come to drink sweet nectar from the beautiful flowers that grow around the village. But once upon a time, the birds did something extra special. Read on...

How to Pronounce It...

Tzintzuntzan sounds like

TSEENT soont SAHN.

Many years ago, a farmer named Isidro lived on the outskirts of Tzintzuntzan with his wife, Consuelo, and their three small children.

Every morning the family would rise at the rooster's first call and go to work side by side in their wheat fields. They cared for their crop until it was ripe and ready to be harvested. When all of the wheat was cut, they sold it to the nearby mill.

One year Isidro and Consuelo planted the seeds as usual for a new crop of wheat. Day after day they searched the sky for rain clouds, but none could be seen. From dawn until dusk the sun shone bright and hot in the sky.

Isidro watched the spindly stalks of wheat in the parched earth slowly wither and turn into yellow straw. Even the hardy cacti growing around the farm turned brown and brittle. The river dried up.

All the flowers withered as well, and the hummingbirds could not find nectar to drink. Many died. "Poor little birds," Consuelo said to Isidro. "We must find a way to help them."

Together they devised a plan. Isidro took the burro and two large clay jars and followed the dry river bed to the lake, which still held a small amount of water. There he filled the jars.

When Isidro returned home, Consuelo carefully mixed the water with clay to mold tiny pots in the shape of flowers. She baked the pots in the sun, and then she and the children painted them with all the bright colours that were once in the garden.

Next Consuelo mixed sugar with the remainder of the water and poured the sweet nectar into the clay containers.

The children placed the painted containers in the branches of the bushes around the garden. Soon a blur of wings surrounded the pots, and the hummingbirds drank their fill.

Isidro struggled to bring fresh water from the lake every day. Consuelo mixed the sweet nectar, and the children made sure the pots were always filled. The hummingbirds were saved!

But as Consuelo watched her children with the little birds, she began to worry. The hummingbirds now had something to eat, but how would she feed her children? There was no wheat to sell and hardly any food in the cupboard.

The hummingbirds, sensing her anxiety, flew out of the bushes and spread over the dusty field like an iridescent blanket. Each bird was a whirl of activity as it gathered a few small bits of straw in its beak and flew back toward Consuelo. When a small pile had formed, the birds settled at her feet and began to work.

As Consuelo looked on, the little birds darted about, weaving the bits of straw into beautiful tiny figures.

Consuelo called to Isidro and the children. "What a blessing this is," she said excitedly. "See how the hummingbirds have shown us what to do!"

She asked Isidro and the children to gather all the straw from the fields and to pile it in the shade by the front porch. Then Consuelo showed them how to weave the figures.

Day and night they wove. Soon the pile of straw was transformed into tiny dancers, musicians, skeletons, and many other shapes.

"We will sell the figures at the Day of the Dead festival!" Isidro proclaimed. "All the villagers will gather in the town square to eat, talk, and explore the marketplace. They will be buying gifts to give to their children and to honour the dead."

On the morning before the festival, the family took their straw figures to the village to sell.

The square was soon crowded with people, and everyone stopped to admire the woven figures. Isidro and Consuelo sold all of them quickly and earned enough money to last all year!

They bought sweets for the children and food, flowers, and candles for the festival.

At midnight, the family joined the rest of the villagers in the procession to the cemetery. There they cleaned their ancestors' graves and placed flowers on the headstones. Then they told the children stories about their grandparents and great-grandparents.

Several weeks later it began to rain. The family laughed and sang because they knew the river would be full again. The wheat would grow and the flowers would blossom for the hummingbirds.

Every year after that, Isidro, Consuelo, and their children wove the straw and displayed the tiny figures. And to this day their children's children and their children remember the hummingbirds' gift. ◆

Congratulations! You've just read two folk tales from faraway lands.

Something to Think About

The Wisdom of Folk Tales

"A trickster must be careful whom he tricks" is the *moral* of *The Man Who Could Transform Himself*. The moral sums up the wise lesson that the tale teaches. What does the moral of this tale mean? Can you think of some modern-day tricksters who should be more careful?

What do you think the moral of *The Hummingbirds' Gift* is? Discuss it with a small group. Write your wisest ideas on the chalkboard.

Wise or Foolish?

The Man Who Could Transform Himself is all about magic. As the story shows, magic powers can be used wisely or foolishly.

- The older brother has the good luck to meet a magician. What promise does the magician ask him to make before he gives him magic powers?

- What is the first magic trick the older brother performs? Is it wise or foolish?

- What clever trick does the older brother play on the rich man?

- What happens when he tries to repeat his trick the next day with the tall man?

- Does the older brother keep his promise to the magician? Explain your answer.

- Why does the magician teach the older brother a lesson? How does he do it?

TIP > Support your answer with details from the folk tales.

Understanding the Story

Helping Others

In the Mexican folk tale, *The Hummingbirds' Gift*, Isidro and Consuelo grow wheat to make a living.

- What misfortune happens to the family?

- Even though they are worried about their wheat, Isidro and Consuelo help the hummingbirds. How?

- When the children become hungry, the birds do something special to help in return. What is it? Why do you think they did it?

- At what Mexican festival does the family sell their straw figures?

- Why will Isidro and Consuelo's children and grandchildren and great-grandchildren never forget the hummingbirds' gift?

YOUR TURN TO WRITE

Storytelling

Storytellers pass on legends and folk tales from one generation to the next.

- Think of stories your family tells over and over. Perhaps they are about things that happened long ago. In groups of four or five, take turns telling and listening to your favourite family stories.

- When you like the way you're telling your story, write it down. Imagine that you are telling the story to a younger child.

TIP ⟩ Dialogue

- Include dialogue in your story. It's fun to read. Here is an example:

> *Elephant flapped his ears, but the buzzing sound wouldn't go away.* "What's that annoying noise?" *he asked.*
>
> "It's me!" *shouted Rabbit in a tiny voice.*
>
> *Elephant looked down, way down to the ground.* "And who are you?" *he bellowed.*